alfredo arribas

works 92→2000

Graphic design:
Quim Nolla

Graphic assistance:
Adrià Nolla
Toni Sánchez
Núria Andreu
(photographs of air traffic control,
Barcelona Airport)

Production:
[di·zain] Barcelona

Introductory texts by
Ignasi de Solà-Morales
(translation by Elaine Fradley)
Project descriptions edited by
Albert Ferré
Documentation compiled by
Toni Sánchez
Cover, virtual model by
Guillermo Grasso

A CIP catalogue record for this book is
available from the Library of
Congress, Washington D.C., USA

Deutsche Bibliothek Cataloging-in-
Publication Data

Alfredo Arribas : works 1992 - 2000.
- Basel ; Boston ; Berlin : Birkhäuser,
2000
ISBN 3-7643-5896-3

© 2000 Birkhäuser – Publishers for
Architecture, P.O. Box 133, CH-4010
Basel, Switzerland
Printed on acid-free paper produced
from chlorine-free pulp. TCF ∞

Printed in Spain
ISBN 3-7643-5896-3

9 8 7 6 5 4 3 2 1

alfredo arribas works

92 → 2000

Introduction by Ignasi de Solà-Morales

Birkhäuser – Publishers for Architecture
Basel · Boston · Berlin

works

the architecture of alfredo arribas

in global culture

Ignasi de Solà-Morales

→ It is a well-known fact that architectural culture produces sets of values and particularly hierarchies of names; at any one time, they form the body of images endorsed by expert opinion and the few names we constantly find invited to take part in high-profile competitions, chosen for institutional commissions for buildings with particular political and social significance, or surrounded by the aura of prizes, nominations or distinctions awarded by a kind of *worldwide academy* which is lauded and publicised in the leading journals or by the fashions adopted at architecture schools the world over.

→ This phenomenon is clearly the result of what we call globalization, taking this term to designate cultural phenomena whose effects extend homogeneously to most of the world's cultural circles.

→ There is of course a more restrictive meaning of the idea of globalization: this is the sense which has been used, for instance, by geo-economists such as Harvey, Castells or Sassen. For them, globalization is ultimately a phenomenon which involves the concentration of decision-making power in a few metropolitan areas of the globe. Over and above regions and states, the globalization which has been produced by the density and flow of communications generates a concentration of power never imaginable in the past with implications for social behaviour and cultural models which were quite unforeseeable just a few years back.

→ But the globalization of economic powers and cultural globalization are very closely linked. One of the most obvious reasons for the localization of these power centres is the availability of new cultural images. The persuasive power of decision-making centers is inevitably linked to the creation of places where the making of images can determine an ideal environment for the demands of economic power in the form of communication density, innovation and services.

→ It is cultural globalization which also constructs a *star system* for architecture, with the *ever-presence* of a small group of architects. In its *academic* form, it is also this phenomenon which leads to the homogenized dissemination of certain formal paradigms which are associated with institutions of high culture, such as museums, universities or prestigious professional publications.

→ We also have to understand the architecture of Alfredo Arribas from the point of view of cultural globalization. But the first issue I would like to address is the difference between his acclaimed production world-wide and the *academy* I refer to above.

→ Before embarking on this analysis, I should like to make it quite clear that my marked interest in the work of this still young architect is due to the fact that he has achieved his prominent name in the world architecture scene by following a different path from what I call the *academic* way, producing a series of works whose significance for contemporary figurative culture cannot be assimilated or even compared to that of the products of the *happy few* I have already often referred to in this text.

→ For me, there is no doubt at all that Arribas' work bears the stamp of globality for the very nature of his commissions, not just because of their geographical distribution. The *themes* of both the works he has produced to date and those which are planned for the near future are, above all, global in content: they invent, unfold, propose architectural forms and languages related to the typical forms of social behaviour and the demands of global, transnational, mediatic, mass culture. But in his case, the content and geographical diversity are not the result of climbing to the peaks of the great names which go to form the new *academy* of today's architecture; they are the result of his intelligent capacity for putting his finger on the pulse of the production circuits of the new culture with the utmost efficiency and creativity. The main interest of his work lies in the fact that it encompasses not just one system but many, and therefore many possible forms of globalization.

→ For this reason, we can only understand the architecture of Alfredo Arribas if we bear in mind that it occupies a prime position in the rapid-fire production of images and architectonic spaces not only being celebrated but also devoured by a cultural network which incorporates architecture in the frenzied world of the mass consumption of images and leisure.

→ The architectural culture of the elite continues to concentrate on architectures which follow the conventional model of the building as a representation of the world order. Sense of place, balance, dialogue between interior and exterior, use of materials according to a tectonic logic, personal expression of a given conception of the spirit of the time – these are just some of the constants of the architecture I refer to as conventional, the production and presence of which continues to determine the characteristics of the contemporary *Gotha*.

→ However, contemporary culture does not end here; on the contrary, it seems to give greater and greater importance to another type of values and content which have little to do with the conventional tradition that has merely been reinterpreted by the modern project. We are in fact dealing with the new culture of the *media*, characterized by two new coordinates.

→ First of all, this new culture is simply part of the changing system of signs which most of the world's citizens use to formalize their interests and priorities. It is of course a mediatized system of signs - that is, one which is codified and transmitted by today's powerful *media*. The architecture of globalization is disseminated by television, cinema and the popular press far more than by the pages of professional journals or high culture programs. It is the co-existence with the repertoires of images used by these mass media as vehicles for their narratives that basically underlies the system of signs of a new architecture irrevocably linked to media phenomena.

→ Secondly, this architecture, as well as intermingling with media culture, also finds an excellent interpretative dimension in it. When Arribas designs the stage for the opening ceremony of the Olympic Games, when he contributes his proposals to an operation to publicize a new product of the motor industry, when he reinterprets the urban image of a hotel or high-rise, his point of departure is neither an enlightened attempt to moralize to people, nor a modernist attempt to order the industrial society of the future. His architecture is immersed in the contradictory world of postmodernity, from the midst of which, with the inventiveness and creativity of his trade, he comes up with spaces for leisure, everyday life, consumerism or rest. What characterizes postmodern culture is the impossibility of distinguishing between economic stimuli and the promptings of desire and longing for gratification as they come gushing out. The architecture produced by this deliberate confusion is, above all, an architecture which outdoes the intentions of conventional architecture on all counts.

→ The difference between Alfredo Arribas' body of work and the projects produced by the big household names lies in the total transparency and reversibility of the former as opposed to the opacity and finality of the work of conventional architects. Transparency of a work which has no complexes about opening up to the energies circulating in the *media*, to their requirements and priorities. Reversibility because it is from inside this global culture, which is visual and tactile, musical and sexual, that his work produces and receives, proposes and adopts, emerges and becomes part of a creative movement which is multiple and nomadic, with nothing linear or unidirectional about it.

→ In general, the world of contemporary architectural criticism has not paid enough attention to the type of products I should like to explain and evaluate here with no ill will whatsoever.

→ For instance, Charles Jencks was mistaken when he turned the evidence of this global phenomenon of postmodern media culture into a *style*, reducing everything that was most genuine about the initial moments of postmodernism to the models which cultural history has traditionally used in an attempt to order and explain the works of each epoch. Reyner Banham, too, confused the effects of globalization as a result of sophisticated communication technologies with the dawn of a new technological age which, figuratively speaking, was to be the inspiration for a form of architecture which worshipped the machine as a permanent paradigm of progress and innovation. Finally, Manfredo Tafuri intuited the changes which were taking place as a bona fide catastrophe. Where his posture went wrong, however, was in anathematizing any chance of a flirtation with the new conditions of late-capitalist culture in the name of classical culture and Hegelian reason.

→ So were these the only possible positions? Did time-honoured architecture have a monopoly on establishing criteria and developing instruments for understanding something which was right before our eyes?

→ Alfredo Arribas' work pinpoints a kind of output which is particularly intelligent and permeable to this contemporary situation of global culture which is, naturally, mediatic, but which also has other characteristic features.

→ The writer of these lines wanted, while adopting the very style of the elitist culture he was criticizing, to re-visit some of the works included in this book. Vain pretension! Although most of the works published here were produced no more than ten years ago, a good many of them no longer exist or have been manipulated, abandoned and stripped of the elements of tension which were their strength. This statement reveals a new argument: that of the ephemeral nature of the type of architecture I wish to deal with here. It is not a question of the architect, in many cases, being contacted to design provisional installations, structures required for an event which has been planned as finite from the beginning. Even in the cases where the most solid materials are used and in programs which will perhaps not change for many years, this type of architecture is, by its very nature, fundamentally ephemeral.

→ At the end of his life, Michel Foucault, who concerned himself with the images, with the architectures which upheld institutions and with the painting which re-presented the supposedly intelligible, rational universe, wrote a text about the works of a contemporary French artist, Fromanger, a particular friend of his. The work of Fromanger, which awoke the aging Foucault's interest, is an example of the manipulation of images and work on them using conventional photographic materials. What interested Foucault was "the indefinite circulation of the images" and the "seizing of events by means of a constant territorialization and deterritorialization of the reality alluded to, rather than their capacity to represent what is real". It may seem rather stale to cite Foucault in this context. I will attempt to show that this is not the case, that the example of the painting of a contemporary artist can also provide us with the keys to an architecture "of the event", as well as to the processes of territorialization and deterritorialization which this architecture is capable of producing.

→ When we refer to the ephemeral nature of Alfredo Arribas' works, it is in the sense of Foucault's reflections on the works of a contemporary painter like Fromanger.

→ Architecture is basically an event which takes place in a time and a place. Understanding the fragility of these conditions is the complete opposite of the approach Mies van der Rohe took when he designed the German Pavilion for the 1929 Barcelona World Fair: an ephemeral building, designed for eternity.

→ Arribas' works of architecture explain, cross, unfold the contingent condition to which their capacity for attraction and stimulation is subject. In other words, his works accept the challenge of designing not for eternity, but for a time, for an intense instant in which the proposal and its fruition joyfully come together. They are not extemporaneous works guided by the wrong clock: on the contrary, they are works which, in the constant flow of media culture, know that seizing the instant, producing the effect, introducing the fold is, perhaps, the best possible response in the archipelago of instants which go to make up our experience.

→ "Territorialize and deterritorialize" points to another no less important case of fragility. Duration having become an instant, is a fragile affair for architecture, too; yet the place, the territory which architecture colonizes, is equally fragile. Globalization has also manipulated the consistency of geography, showing us that we live in many places at once and explaining that any one place is not so much a permanence as the result of a productive will. This is, effectively, an architecture which rests on Deleuze's one thousand plateaux, in places which exist just as long as does the constituent energy of the architecture that gives them their consistency.

→ One of the things which most invites reflection about the work of Alfredo Arribas is its real geographical dispersion, a dispersion which goes practically hand-in-hand with the sense of no-place, of the non-urban – both landscaped and natural – in which his buildings are placed.

→ Another characteristic feature of his body of work is the centrifugal force governing his projects, extending them beyond themselves or closing them in, like a snail's shell, in a condition of exclusive interiors.

→ Which territory corresponds to this architecture? In my opinion, all and none. The organization of the works brought together in this book is apparently based on a series of locations: Barcelona, the Far East, Germany,... Europe, perhaps. This mnemonic classification is useful but doesn't quite manage to convince us that each of his projects is determined by its geography. By culture, maybe. By mass cultural consumption in its different manifestations in various world societies. The territorialization which Arribas sets out is marked by cultural operators, by the distribution of consumers, but in no way does it correspond to place or landscape understood as a fixed point in geography or memory.

→ The various projects are pervaded by an extreme artificiality which is lucidly assumed, their *no-place* explaining the territorial crisis of the contemporary metropolis.

→ I should like to close these reflections with a final, very general observation.

→ In an architecture like the body of work presented here, who is the architect? At the start of this article, I attempted to distinguish between the type of architecture I termed *academic* or conventional and the architecture produced by artists such as Alfredo Arribas. I tried to clarify that this difference was by no means a value judgement, or, if it was, perhaps it was one which aimed to show a particular interest and enthusiasm for an attitude which appeared to be very much in synergy with the conditions of global culture.

→ This approach has major consequences, even from a practical point of view.

→ The production of aesthetic messages in mass culture is a field in which only the convergence of very varied agents can produce outstanding results.

→ The works of Alfredo Arribas are backed by sponsors, proprietors, investors, who can all count from the outset on the complicity of other image-production professionals. In architecture's conventional working method, the client – the patron – evidently requires the architect to interpret the messages of power, monumentality and permanence to which he or she is invited to give concrete form.

→ In the architecture we are looking at here, it is impossible to separate the initiative of the sponsor and the production of ideas by the architect from the management of these ideas and the specific contributions of consultants or experts invited to take part in the overall construction of the product.

→ As far back as the thirties, Walter Benjamin foresaw that the cinema, as an industry which produced reproducible works of art, was tending to *socialize* production, fusing the contributions of individuals – the director, cameraman, editor, actors and so on – in a system of complex interaction which characterizes the work of art in modern times. The work of Alfredo Arribas shown here – it would be absurd to deny it – has the stamp of his central role and sensibilities as well as the presence of his recurring motifs and obsessions. But what sets it apart from conventional architecture is the fact that, in a much broader dimension, his is a body of work which demands from the outset to be understood as having gestated with the complicity and the conflicts with other agents of media culture. However, this gestation does not take place *in vitro*, in a space of free creation; it comes into being as a consequence of continual transactions, of an on-going organization of forms, resources and effects. As a result of an invention which is not just formal, but also practical and productive.

→I am convinced that we are looking at a series of works where the linear process of *client-resources-design-construction* cannot be applied. What is set before us here is all the convulsed beauty, the fascination of an unbounded imagination, the immense capacity for bringing together the known and the unknown, the beautiful and the hideous, the worlds of waking and sleep. Its whole fascinating flow of stimuli and perceptions is inseparable from a way of managing products and works which no longer has anything to do with the conventional professional relationship. Quite the opposite: it is a way of producing architecture on the basis of the provisional nature of an instant and the necessity, at each one of these instants, of trying to reflect the unstoppable process of a society dominated by the spectacle of consumerism and the fetishism of merchandise. A global society in which the promise of happiness is associated with the holiday that is free time, with the ceremony of consumerism and the endless extravagance of images and forms, representations and architectures.

→Ignasi de Solà-Morales.

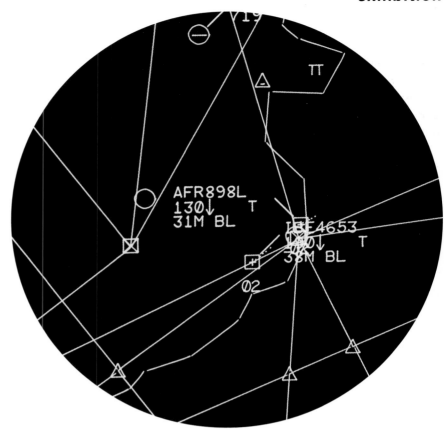

barcelona after 92

→ The conventional distinction between public and private is gradually being dissolved. In the contemporary city, spaces of over-exposure are doubly public. Stadiums, festivals, spaces for music, having a drink and time out, are all much more public than traditional squares and streets.

Activity becomes a spectacle and the presence of people becomes a representation of themselves, for themselves. Expressionist architecture – Poelzig, Scharoun, the later Wright – understood that large containers are theatrical places. The ritual of the museum, the opera house, or the Philharmonic becomes a total spectacle which makes all of us active; we are all actors and spectators in an up-dated version of the total work of art. In the elements designed for the opening ceremony of the Olympic Games, in the play of ramps and movement of Gran Velvet, everything is a spectacle: from the podium for the Olympic opening address to the transformation of wash basins and toilet amenities into a ritualised space of movement where only the hedonism of the hot baths of the ancient world can provide us with a clue as to how personal, intimate hygiene can also become an explicit activity and be made part of a total spectacle.

One of the most reiterated formal techniques in this type of space is the inclusion of heavily pregnant forms, boxes, spheres, ovals, run through by tangential flows or penetrated by corridors which at once incorporate and violate them.

All manner of sexual chords are struck in artificial spaces for night-time leisure. Bodies, looks, seduction, exposure and contact are there from the start, forming part of the iconography which unfolds in these places. The dream of personal fulfillment and of its dissolution in the multitude are present here as extreme poles searching for a tense, moribund compatibility.

Leisure is activity, the space of the spectacle is the pure projection of energies.

***Sceneries and architectonic elements for the opening and closing
ceremonies of the Barcelona Olympic Games (1992)***

 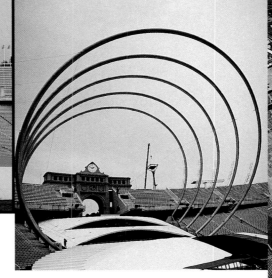 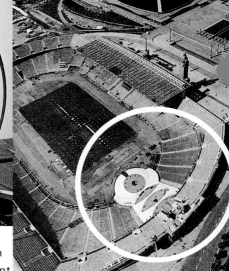

→The staging of the opening and closing ceremonies of the 1992 Summer Olympics was seen as an opportunity to reclaim some of the monumentality and formal simplicity that the old 1925 stadium had lost with its complex renovation by architects Gregotti, Correa, Milà, Margarit and Buxadé. A system of circular platforms reminiscent of the Olympic rings steps up from the athletics field – which was lowered from its original position in order to extend the tiered seating – and reestablishes the lost connection with the old Marathon door and the statues on either side of it. Conceived both as a stage and a backstage, the platforms – a wooden frame structure built in Switzerland and reassembled in the stadium – allow for the magical emergence of the actors and for the staging of tall lighting poles and other supporting elements.

↑ From right to left: Aerial view of the stage in the Olympic stadium, first proposal of a set of ring structures above the stage to support the lighting, and the built proposal, in which these rings are replaced by a series of independent metal poles.

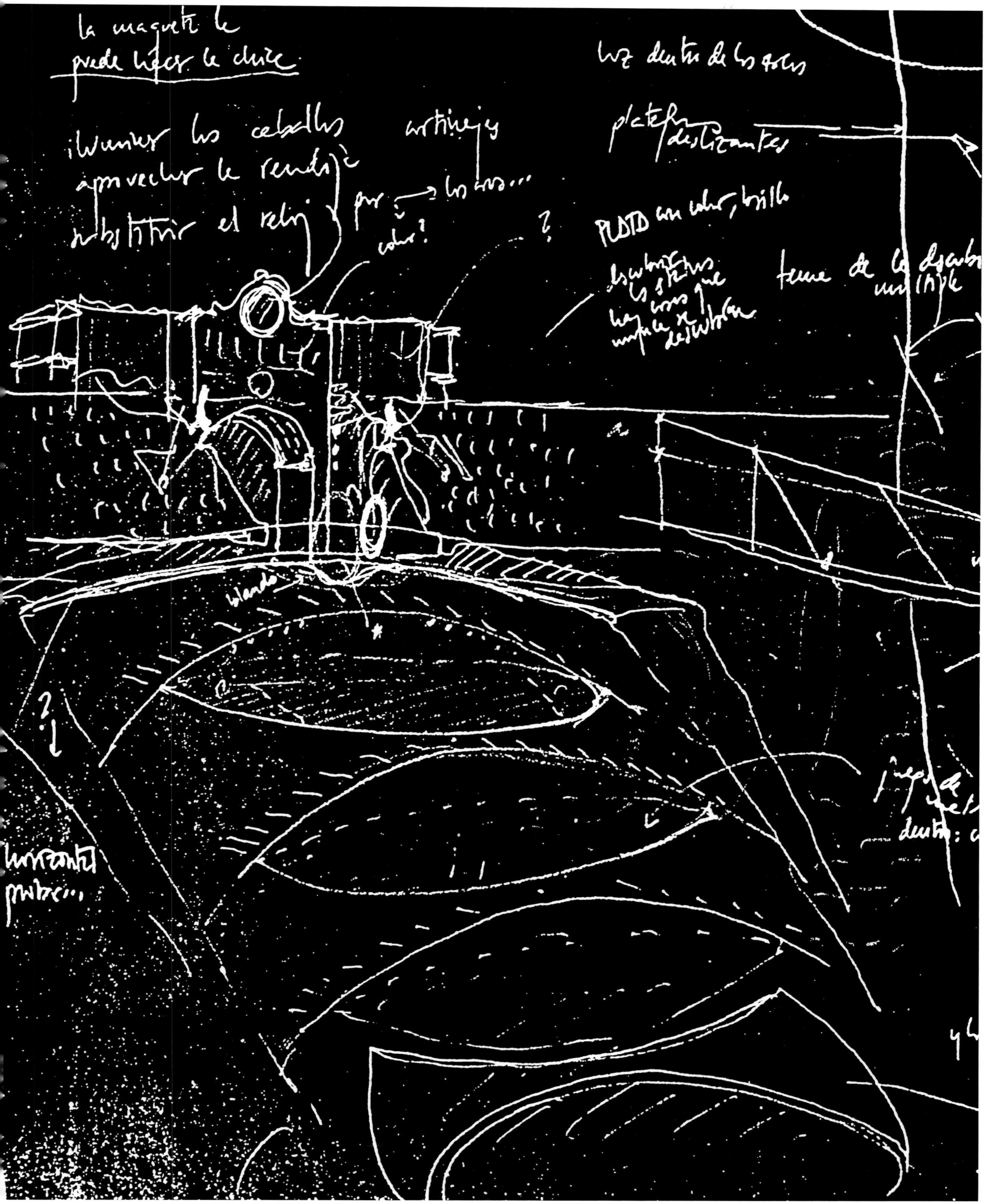

The stage's wooden frame construction assembled in Switzerland.
→ Live TV images of the opening ceremony.

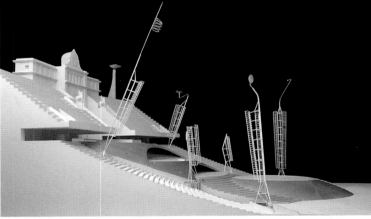

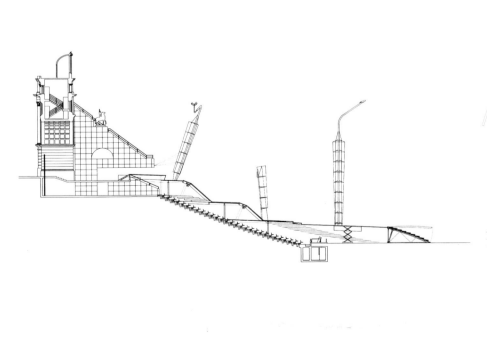

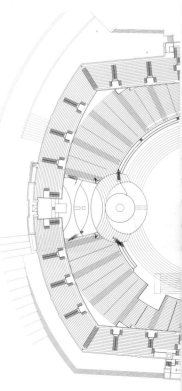

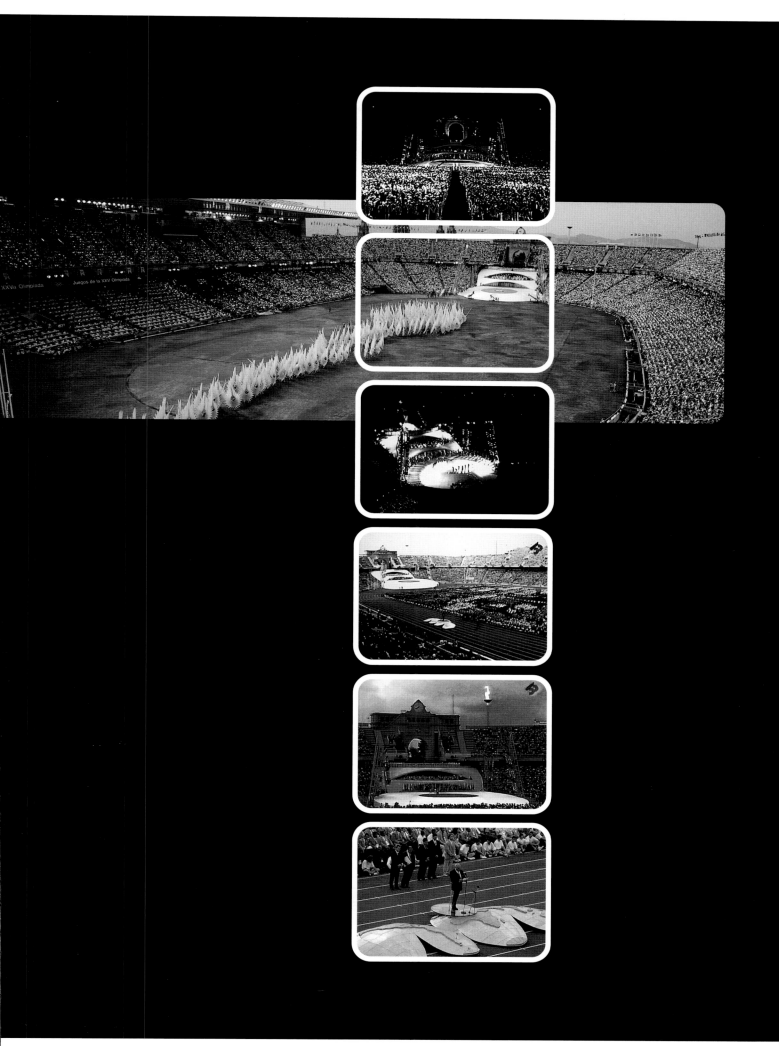

furest

Interior renovation of a fashion store. Barcelona (1992)

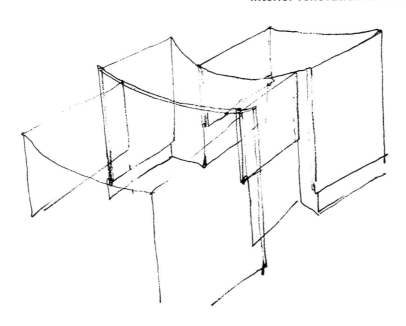

→ This project has been primarily conceived as a continuation – and second example – of the Furest stores designed during the previous decade by the architects Federico Correa and Alfonso Milà – the utmost representatives of what has been called the Barcelona school in architecture. The formal and technological restraints that characterize this period of Catalan architecture, as well as the emphasis it places on contextual references and material simplicity, are reinterpreted here from the perspective of a more exuberant, less academic design approach.

The existing long, narrow, irregular and dark space available for this store – typical of Barcelona turn-of-the-century blocks – is given new qualities with the uniformizing use of a few materials and a new convex, awning-like white ceiling. The basement, with its floor completely clad in dark wood and with an extensive use of mirrors, is given the character of a hidden, private cabinet.

Sketch of the awning-like ceiling.
Cross section showing the two levels.
Floor and ceiling plans of ground floor.
Staircase to the lower floor.

medinaceli

Renovation of a 19th-century palace into the headquarters of a shipping company. Barcelona (1990-1994)

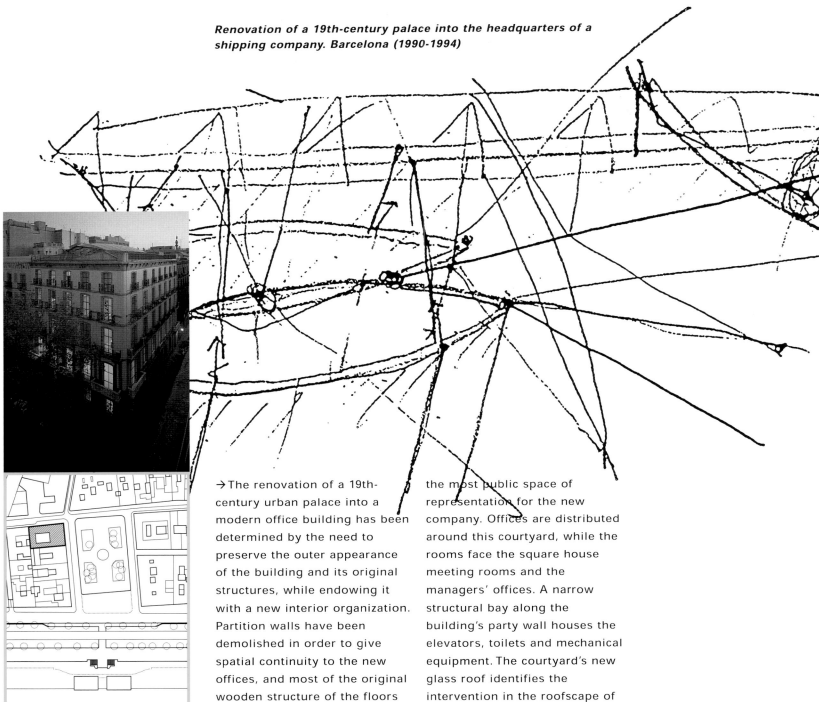

Site plan. The building defines one of the corners of the Plaça del Duc de Medinaceli opening onto the old city's harbour.

→The renovation of a 19th-century urban palace into a modern office building has been determined by the need to preserve the outer appearance of the building and its original structures, while endowing it with a new interior organization. Partition walls have been demolished in order to give spatial continuity to the new offices, and most of the original wooden structure of the floors has been substituted by concrete slabs which incorporate mechanical installations. The building's central courtyard, formerly only a void bringing daylight and air to the interior rooms, has been covered and transformed into the container of a new hanging staircase, and the most public space of representation for the new company. Offices are distributed around this courtyard, while the rooms face the square house meeting rooms and the managers' offices. A narrow structural bay along the building's party wall houses the elevators, toilets and mechanical equipment. The courtyard's new glass roof identifies the intervention in the roofscape of this old neighborhood.

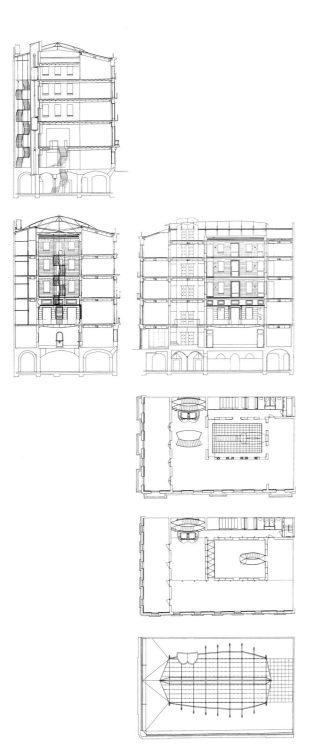

←Sections and floor plans of the
project, from bottom to top: entrance,
typical floor, and roof.
←Cross section and typical floor plan
before renovation.
↑Entrance to the elevator tower and
side staircase. On the right, view of
the large wing facing the street on the
top floor.
→Views of the central courtyard with
the hanging staircase.

sanson

Panoramic hall, bar, and gallery in a former concrete plant. Barcelona (1990-1991)

← The site. The remains of the concrete factory are surrounded by Ricardo Bofill's Walden 7 apartments and his office.
→ Views of the uncompleted new silos and restaurant platform.

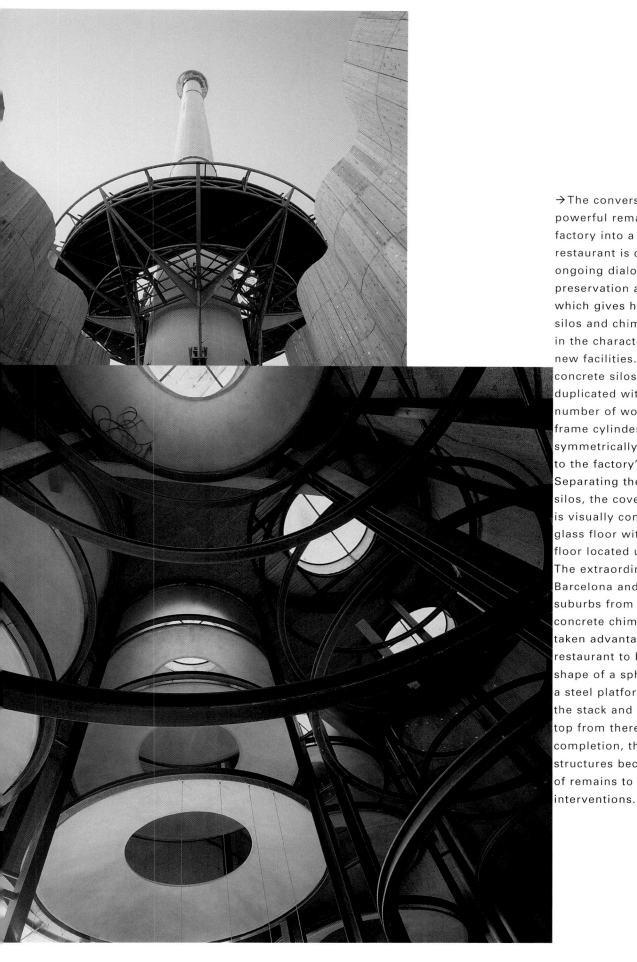

→ The conversion of the powerful remains of a cement factory into a dance club and a restaurant is characterized by an ongoing dialogue between preservation and invention which gives here the factory's silos and chimney a leading role in the characterization of the new facilities. The existing concrete silos have been duplicated with an identical number of wood-cladded, steel-frame cylinders, which were symmetrically placed in relation to the factory's tall chimney. Separating the old and new silos, the covered entrance hall is visually connected through a glass floor with the club's dance floor located underground. The extraordinary views over Barcelona and its western suburbs from the top of the tall concrete chimney were to be taken advantage of in the restaurant to be built in the shape of a spherical skullcap on a steel platform at the base of the stack and then raised to the top from there. Stopped short of completion, the new steel structures become a new layer of remains to be used in future interventions.

↙ The existing silos and chimney.
↓ Plan of the entrance floor and cross section.

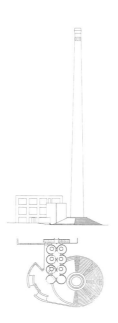

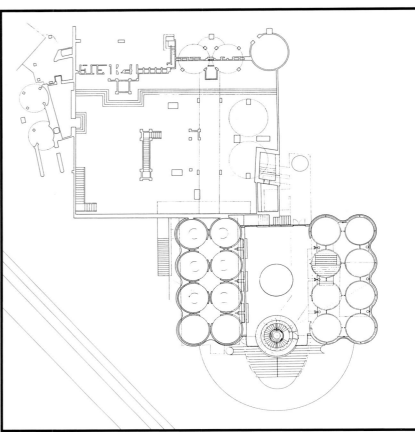

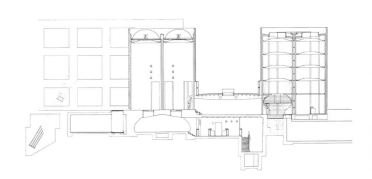

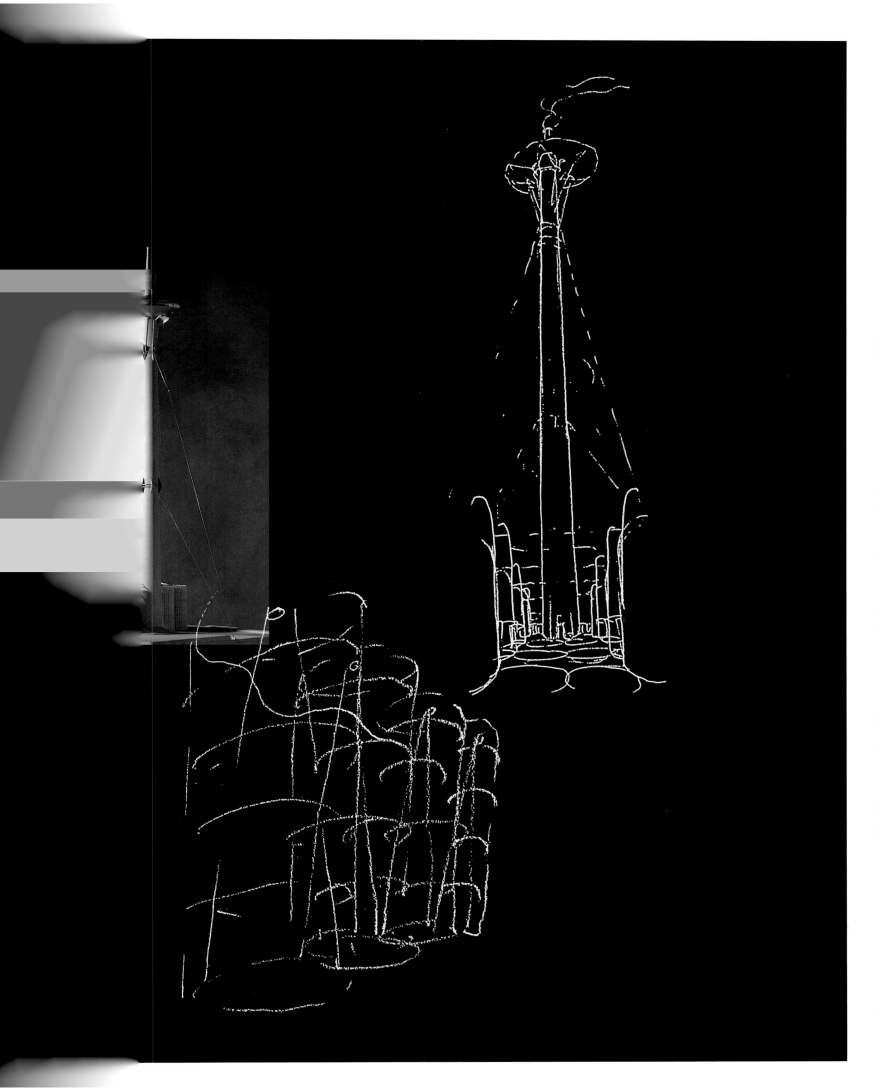

Bar, restaurant, club. Barcelona (1991-1993)

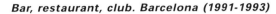

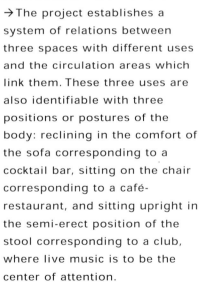

→ The project establishes a system of relations between three spaces with different uses and the circulation areas which link them. These three uses are also identifiable with three positions or postures of the body: reclining in the comfort of the sofa corresponding to a cocktail bar, sitting on the chair corresponding to a café-restaurant, and sitting upright in the semi-erect position of the stool corresponding to a club, where live music is to be the center of attention.

The new club-bar-restaurant broadly respects the original shell of a preexisting garage, although a new basement was excavated and the roofs partially replaced. The ceilings have a complex geometry which combines free plaster forms with sets of perforated metal panels which provide an increased expression of height, and break the simplicity of the original volumes.

The insulating perimeter walls are made of concrete, whereas the interior partitions are minimal and mostly made of steel. The use of wood and rush matting in the floors adds new material qualities to the space and allows for a more clear manifestation of the building's aging. In the basement, a cluster of identical doors brings together toilets, offices, cloakrooms and other storage spaces.

←Sketch and views of the street entrance.
↓Clockwise from bottom left: ramp leading from the street
entrance to the café-restaurant, the club, and the cocktail bar.

↗ Plans and cross section of the building before renovation.
↓ From left to right: cross sections, plan of basement floor (billiard room, toilets, storage and mechanical rooms), ground floor (cocktail bar and club), and upper floor (café-restaurant and kitchen). The model illustrates the spatial relationships between the different parts of the project.

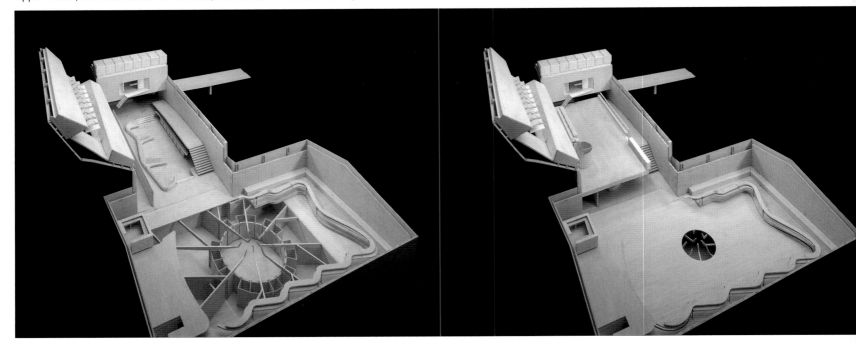

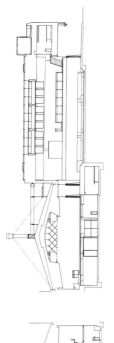

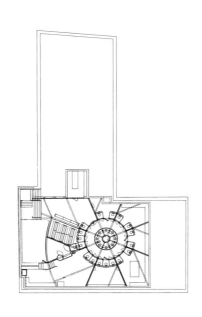

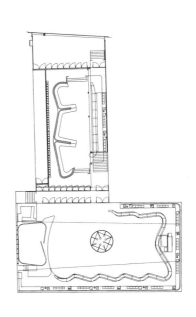

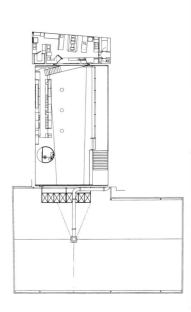

↗ View from the cocktail bar of the ramp and stairs connecting the entrance with the café-restaurant on the upper floor and with the club in the back.
→ View of the basement space connecting the billiard room, the entrance to the toilets, and a view up into the club.

Views of the club and of the toilets underneath.

The cocktail bar (left) and the restaurant above.

gran velvet

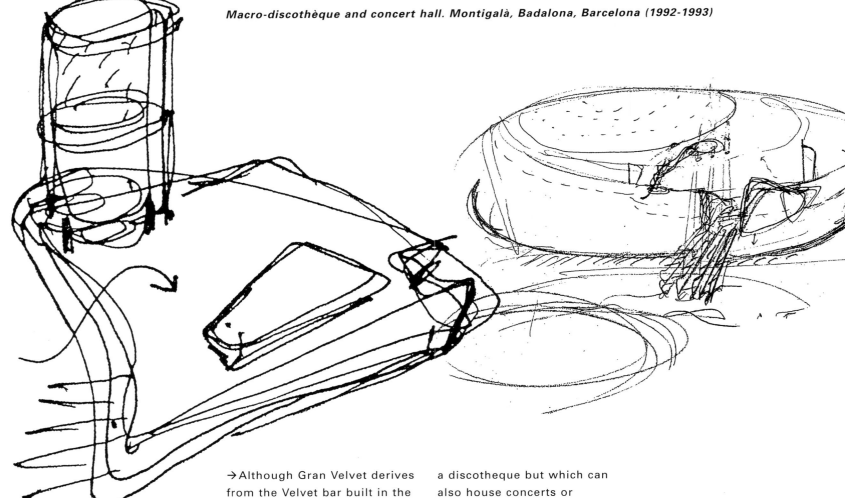

Macro-discothèque and concert hall. Montigalà, Badalona, Barcelona (1992-1993)

→Although Gran Velvet derives from the Velvet bar built in the center of Barcelona in 1987, little resemblance can be found between the two. Gran Velvet is located on a sloping site east of the city, adjacent to one of the city's ring roads and surrounded by warehouses and empty plots. Conceived on a much larger scale than its predecessor, it becomes an ephemeral landmark in this moving peripheral landscape. It is a steel container used primarily as a discotheque but which can also house concerts or conferences – a multipurpose space conceived as a mechanism that links multiple uses and spatial situations. Its two main floors revolve around a large elliptical void which exposes a dance floor, a stage, and connecting ramps and stairs. Long bars, toilets and other facilities are located along the perimeter walls. Above the stage, a 24-meter high tower extends the void beyond the roof, and, paired with a smaller cylinder, becomes the building's most distinctive feature. Inside the smaller tower, the heart of the original Velvet bar, literally reproduced and sealed in glass, is a curious witness to its own transformation.

↑ Site plan showing the proximity of the freeway.
Cross sections through the towers and model showing the interior layout.

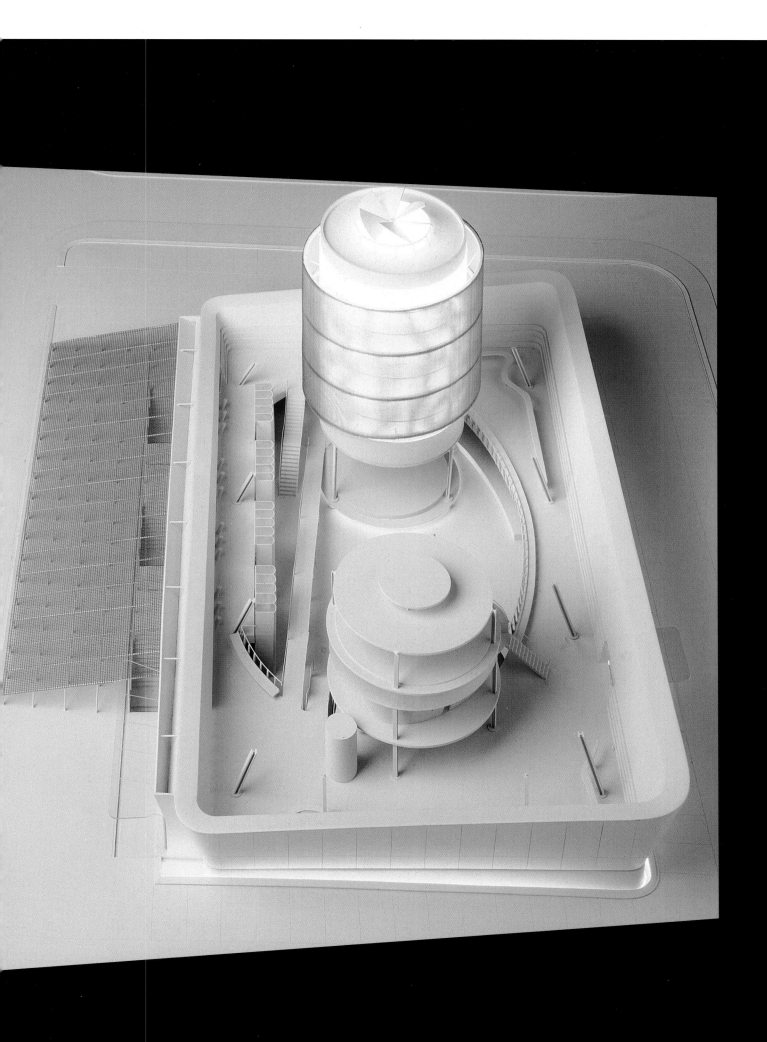

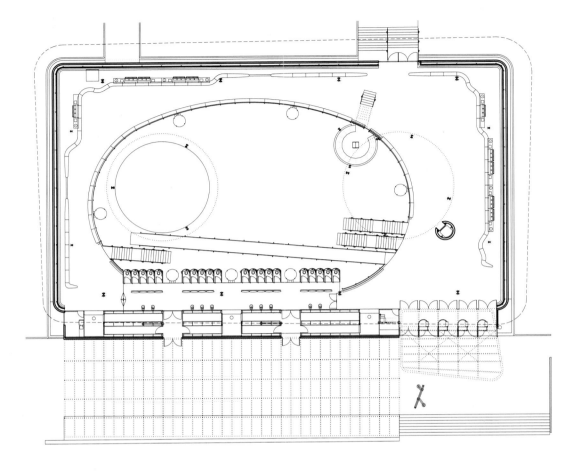

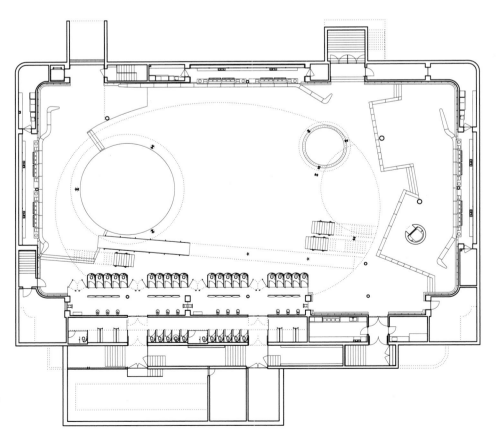

Clockwise from bottom left: plans of the dance floor, intermediate access level, old Velvet bar in the second tower, office above.

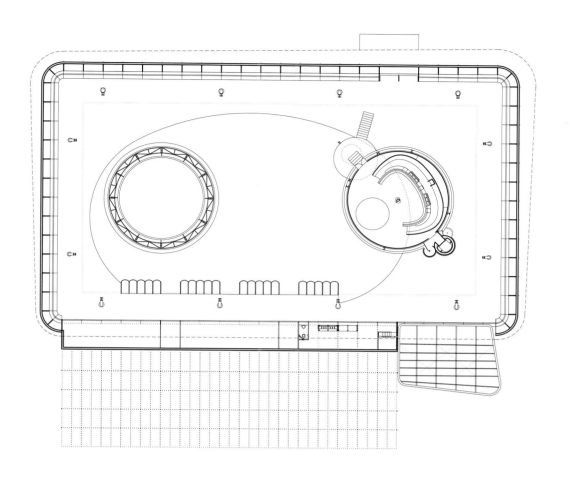

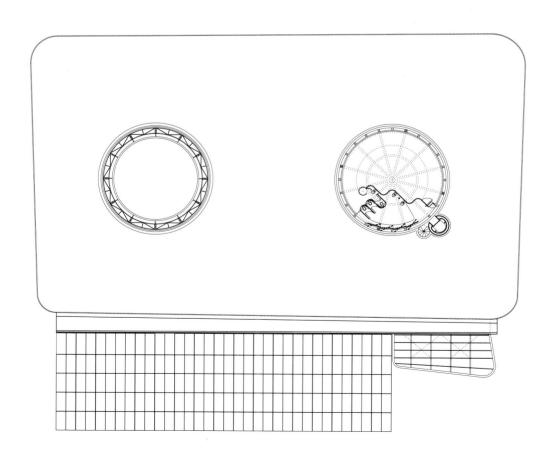

Views of the steel-frame construction.

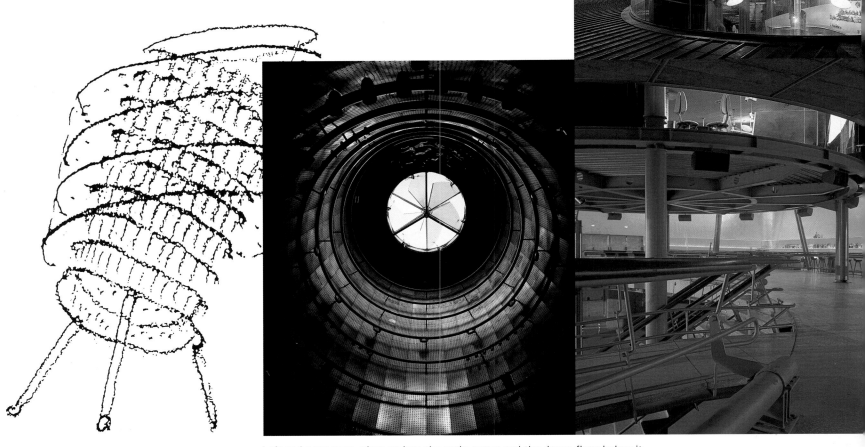

Left and next page, view up into the main tower and the dance floor below it.
Right, views of the entrance space and of the second tower with the old Velvet bar
reproduced inside.

Above, views of the dance floor and the perimeter bars. Below, the upper mezzanine at entrance level and the connecting stairs and ramp. The cylindrical aluminum panels hide the toilets and service areas.

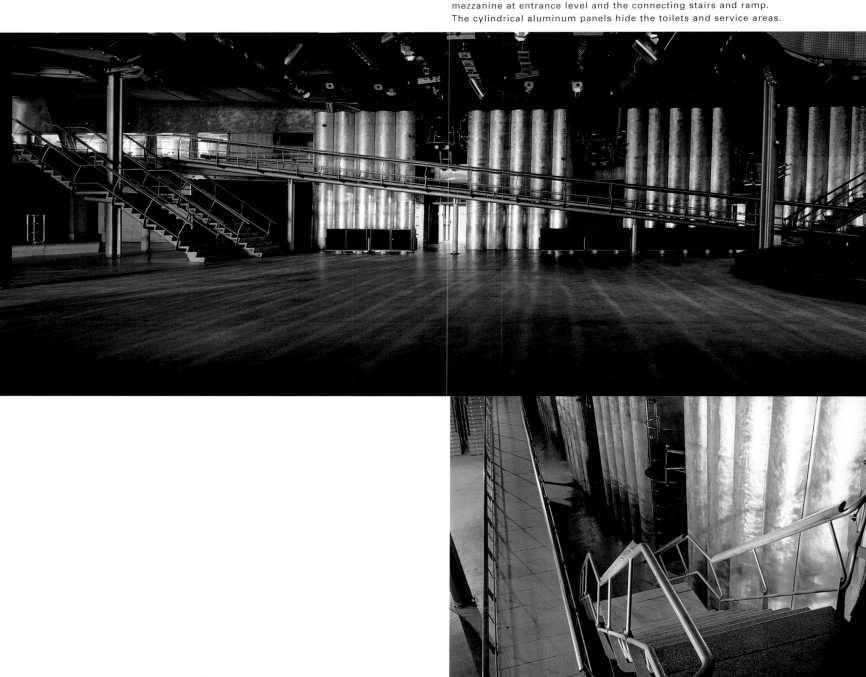

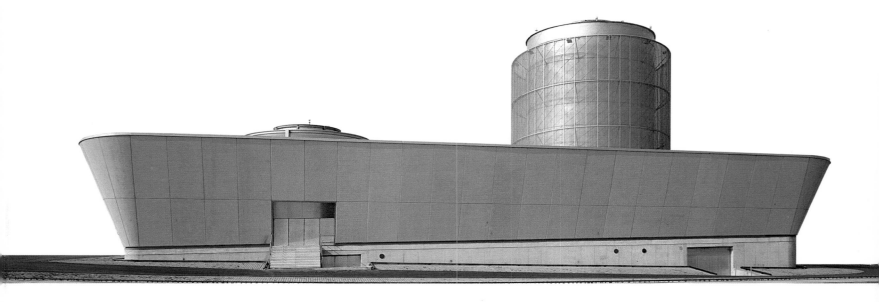

Clockwise from top left: views from south, north, and northeast (entrance).

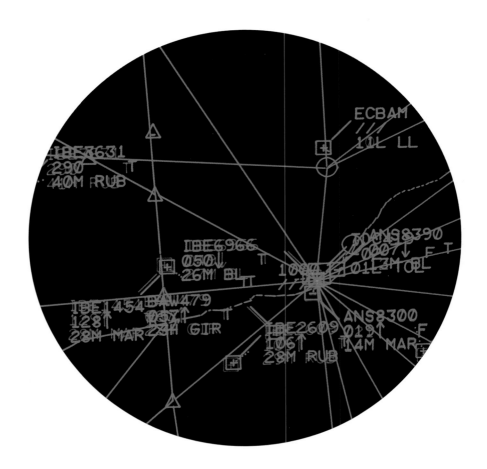

far(?)east

→ Which city are these buildings for? Landmarks in an emerging, chaotic landscape. Lofty vantage points which command bustling, fragmented, panoramic views where arbitrary, additive building extends out of sight. The richest construct of the gaze as an isolated activity is landscape. From a remote viewpoint, through the mediation of the picture in the past, and of the photograph or the picture window in the present, the contemplation of diversity can become an inexhaustible attraction for the sense of sight. The landscape as an autonomously created aesthetic experience is the result of independent construction by the subject of the culture of the Enlightenment. The conversion of the urban into landscape, taking the utmost in artificial to the very limits of the experience of nature, is a characteristic form of postmodern culture. The natural landscape and the urban landscape have no center, no reference point around which an order can be established. As opposed to the fixed eye of the Renaissance perspective, the landscape eye wanders, is *distracted*, loses itself in detail or segmental effects. Architecture that is based on the erratic sensibility of the landscape gaze is obliged to either construct landmarks, fixed points, centers around which to order chaos or, conversely, to exploit the experience of inexhaustible time by letting the stimulated eye wander here and there through a vast array of signals which randomly lead it from one spot to another.

A landscape gaze can use two formal repertoires: fluidity or accumulation.

The fluid forms of buildings invite a strolling approach, not stopping, wandering with no set aim, experiencing the sublime sensations of the erratic, the unfinished, through the eye. The dissected forms, the ground plans of buildings divided and then subdivided again, with mechanisms for further fragmentation, multiple symmetries and repetitive addition, extend unchecked; at the opposite extreme is the anxiety vis-à-vis the infinitely small, dissectable, divisible, without ever reaching a limit or an end.

marugame hirai museum

**Contemporary Spanish art museum and office building.
Takamatsu (1991-1993)**

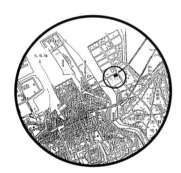

→ The double and contradictory role of the building, as both a landmark dominating an extensive exurban landscape and as a neutral background for three-dimensional artworks, sums up the nature of this architectural idea. As an object, its genesis is a geometrical divertimento, in which the oval outline expands to create a rising contour and, in the lower levels, vigorous cuts on inclined planes create new surfaces of metal trim in the wrapping of colored concrete. Taken as a frame or neutral background, the building features a gigantic suspended curtain wall of steel mesh, joining all the windows into one single frame, and serving as a visual filter of the activities carried on inside. A fringe of low pavilions running parallel to one of the main streets houses the service facilities of a newspaper as well as a cafeteria and a showroom for temporary exhibits.

While the interiors were to have been used mainly as offices by the communications company that owns the building and for cultural activities, when construction was nearly complete, it was decided to turn the lower floors into a unique collection of works of contemporary Spanish art. The building has withstood with dignity this felicitous broadening of its initial aims. Now a container, now the content itself, the project will hopefully continue in the future to benefit from the at once contradictory and fruitful sequence of alternations.

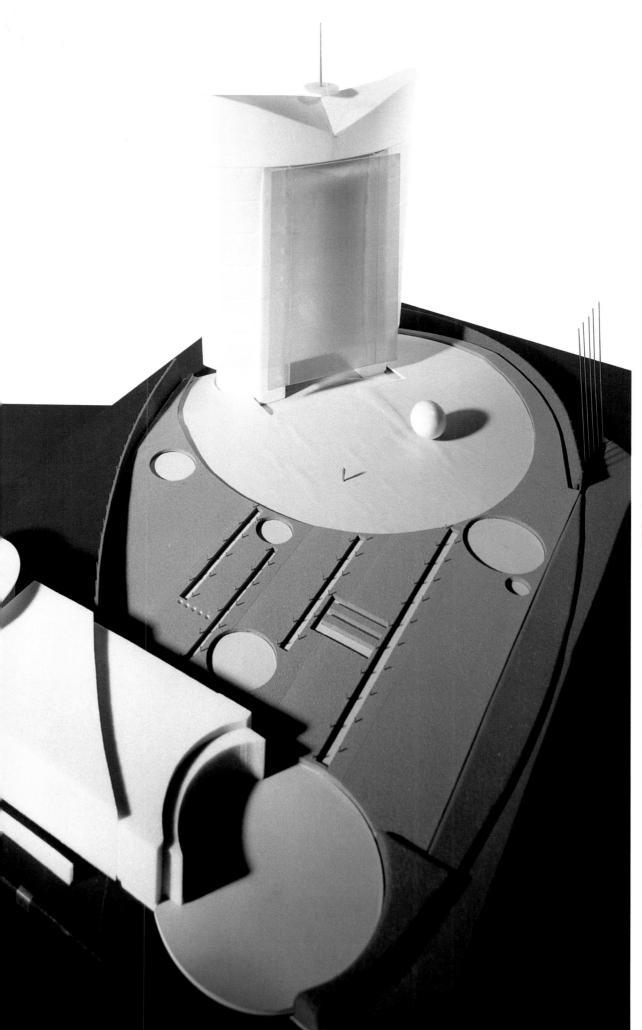

View of the museum as a landmark in the city's skyline.
The model and the aerial photograph show the unifying relatioship established between the different parts of the project by the oval trace.

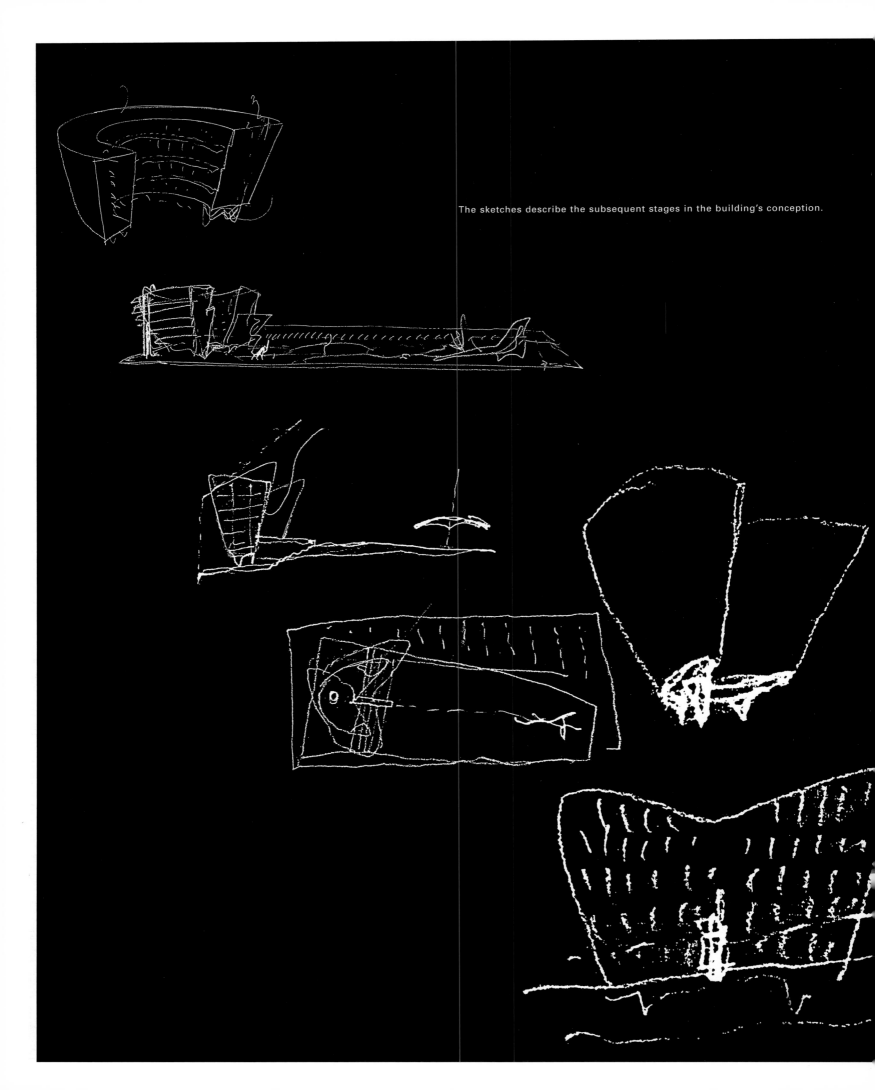

The sketches describe the subsequent stages in the building's conception.

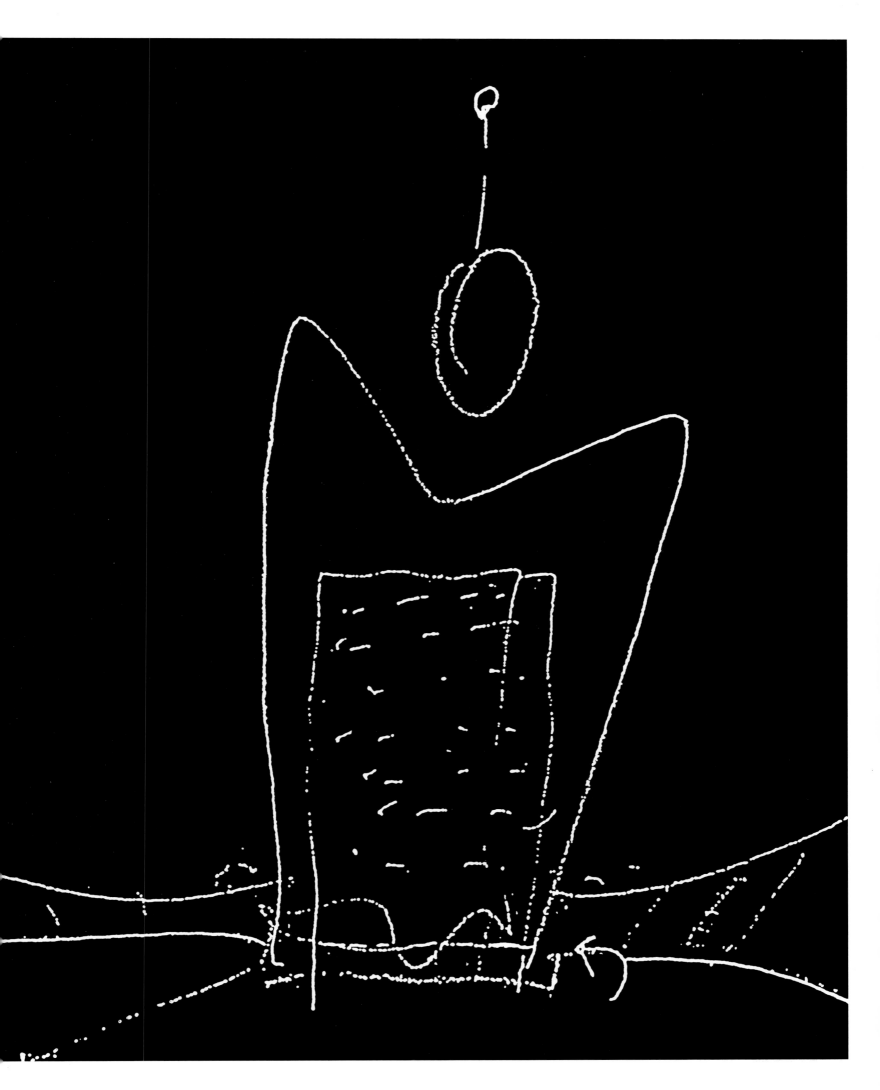

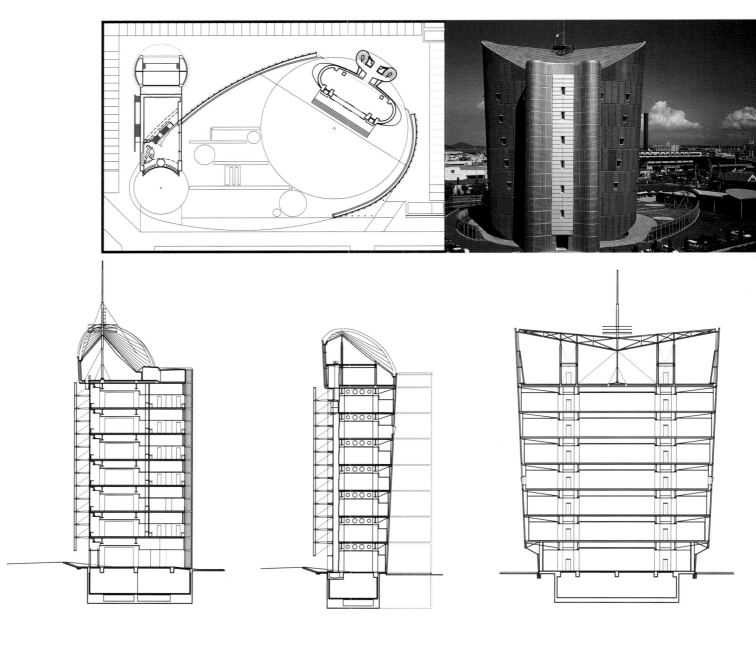

↗Overall plan and views of the southern and northern façades.
↑Cross sections through the staircase, a side wing, and along a major axis
of the elliptical plan. Below, plan of a typical floor.

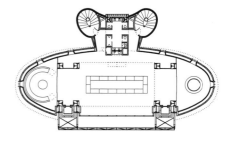

Views of the metal screen on the main façade, which acts as a filter for the activities carried out inside the building. The entrance space is located underneath.

Axonometric views of the ground floor and roof,
showing the structural frames which define the tower's
sculptural base and top cuts.

Exterior and interior views of the staircase shafts.

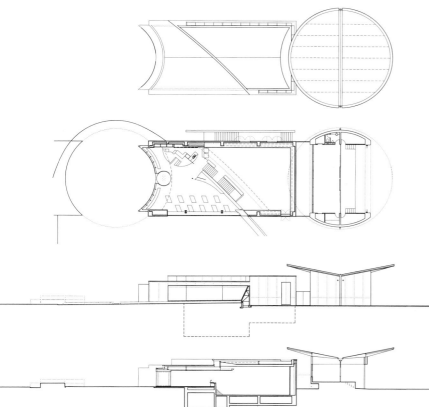

↑In the center of the mediating lawn, a sculpture by Pello Irazu
establishes a distant dialogue with the main building.
←Left page, view of the cafeteria and the gallery for
temporary exhibits looking out on the garden and the main building.
The roof planes and openings reveal the geometrical layout.
←Plans, elevation, and section of the newspaper logistics pavilion
and the wing that houses the cafeteria and the gallery for temporary
exhibitions and also marks the entrance to the museum premises.

Interior design of a golf club house. Choyoda, Tokyo (1991-1992)

→ The brief called for the interior architecture of a new golf club house designed in what was conceived to be an interpretation of traditional Spanish-style architecture. The challenge here was to respond in a coherent way to what was expected from the architects – to provide a modern and more local reinterpretation of this historical thematization. While the spirit and atmosphere of the architectural quotation is reflected in the wide walls, the large rooms, and the great windows, the nature of the container is counteracted by ceilings modeled with vaults, inclined planes, and skylights that introduce new spatial configurations. The applied decoration of coffers and reliefs on the walls exposes the industrial nature of their production and the systematization of the construction methods, thus transforming the initial revivalism into a continuous play between technology and craftsmanship. A selection of furniture from contemporary Spanish designers complements the interiors.

Views of different spatial configurations deriving from the modeling of the plaster ceilings, and samples of applied surface textures.

↑ View of the entrance hall and the ceiling´s steel-frame, which emphasizes the geometrical layout of the plan and filters the view of the original wooden beams.
↗ Cross sections: general floor plan and ceiling plan (above).
↖ View of the meeting room.

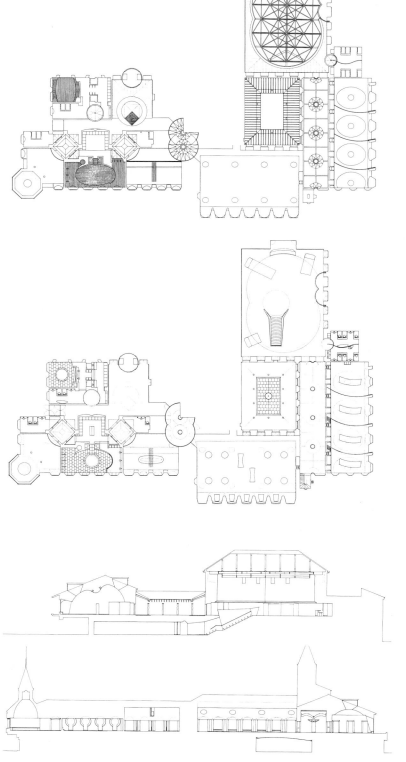

acuarinto

Children's experimental and play park. Nagasaki (1992-1993)

With Javier Mariscal

→ This children's play park occupies the wide interior space of what is outwardly defined as a row of traditional Dutch houses in Huis den Bosch, a theme park near Nagasaki. In a new exercise in stylistic thematization the scale of this large interior with a high pitched roof and two parallel rows of columns is reduced by means of a vertical subdivision which revolves around a central unitary game installation. Access is made via a flight of steps into a mezzanine floor in the form of a perimeter balcony, where the building structure is transformed into a forest of copper pyramids with TV monitors set among them, revealing a multiplicity of images of the secluded world below. A spiral ramp leads the visitors into the ground level which – following the example of the programmatically related Click dels Nens built in Barcelona in 1989 – is centrally occupied by a labyrinth of perspex water tanks made in collaboration with artist Javier Mariscal. The geometry and materialization of the labyrinth creates a fantasy land-/seascape made of reflections, transparencies and concealments. Around it, individual sets of interactive video games occupy the perimeter spaces.

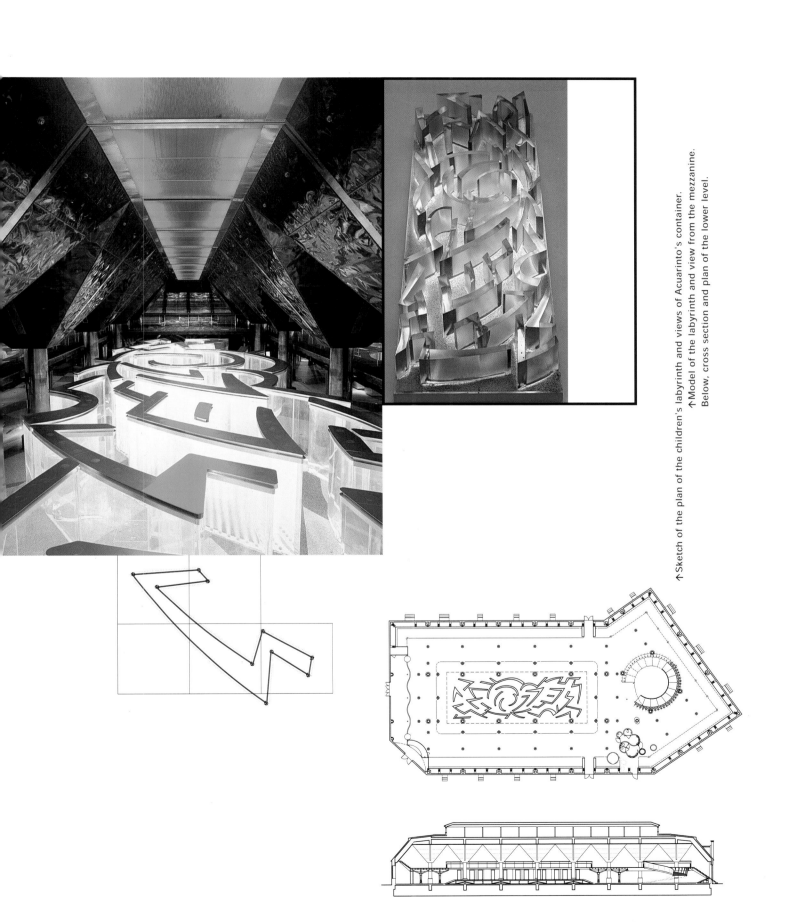

↑Sketch of the plan of the children's labyrinth and views of Acuarinto's container.
↑Model of the labyrinth and view from the mezzanine.
Below, cross section and plan of the lower level.

murasaki river hotel

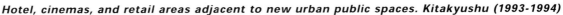

Hotel, cinemas, and retail areas adjacent to new urban public spaces. Kitakyushu (1993-1994)

→ This unrealized project was part of an urban renewal plan called "My Town, My River" for the reclaimed banks of the Murasaki river in central Kitakyushu and would have included the creation of pedestrian and green areas along the riverfront. Strategically located next to the town hall, the city library by Arata Isozaki, and a major bridge, the Murasaki River Hotel formally mimics a neighboring building across the street to define a symmetrical disposition of buildings at the end of the bridge as one of the central city's main gates. In a reference to the surrounding urban fabric and to the flowing greenish river, the building is made up of two white towers at the ends and two slender bands whose façades are clad in green copper. A long, deep void runs between these, separating them and acting as a public skylit atrium and the building's central spine. Vertically, the building is also divided in two different sections, with public amenities and shopping areas connected to the riverbank and a standard hotel programme in the upper floors.

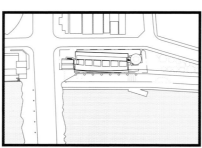

Aerial views of the site adjacent to one of the city's main bridges.
Above, working models showing the design evolution.

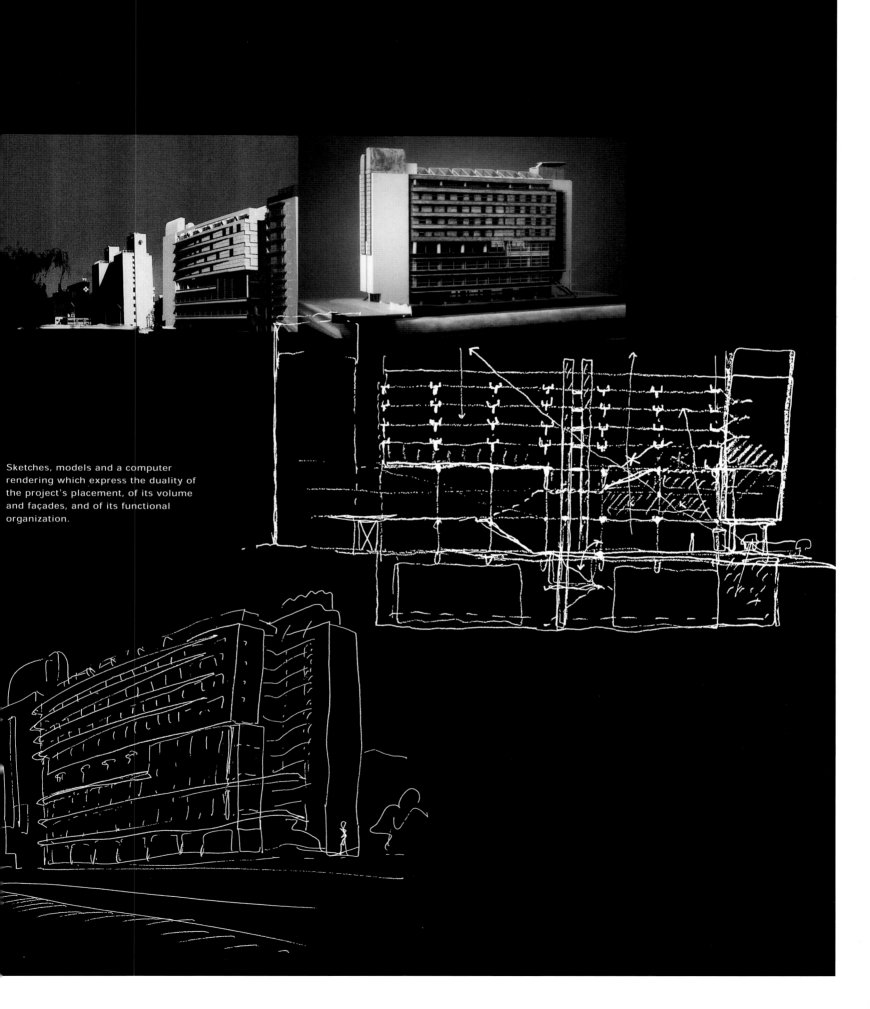

Sketches, models and a computer rendering which express the duality of the project's placement, of its volume and façades, and of its functional organization.

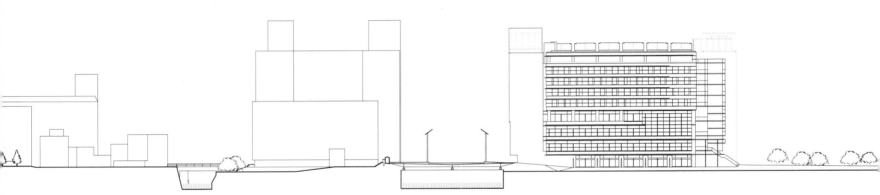

Elevation and cross section of the building in its urban context.

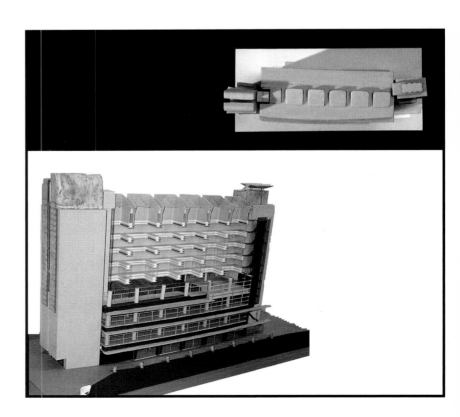

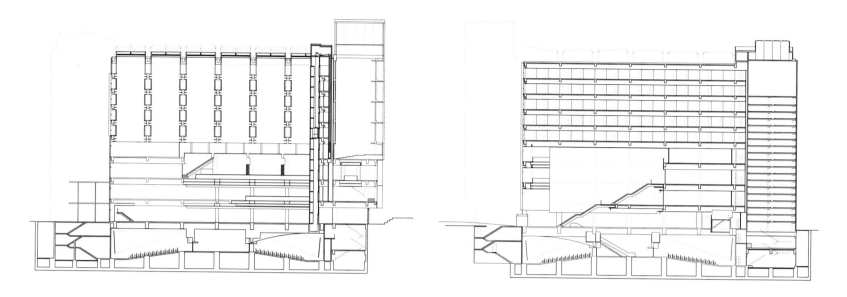

River-side and street-side elevations, and cross sections showing the building's functional layering.

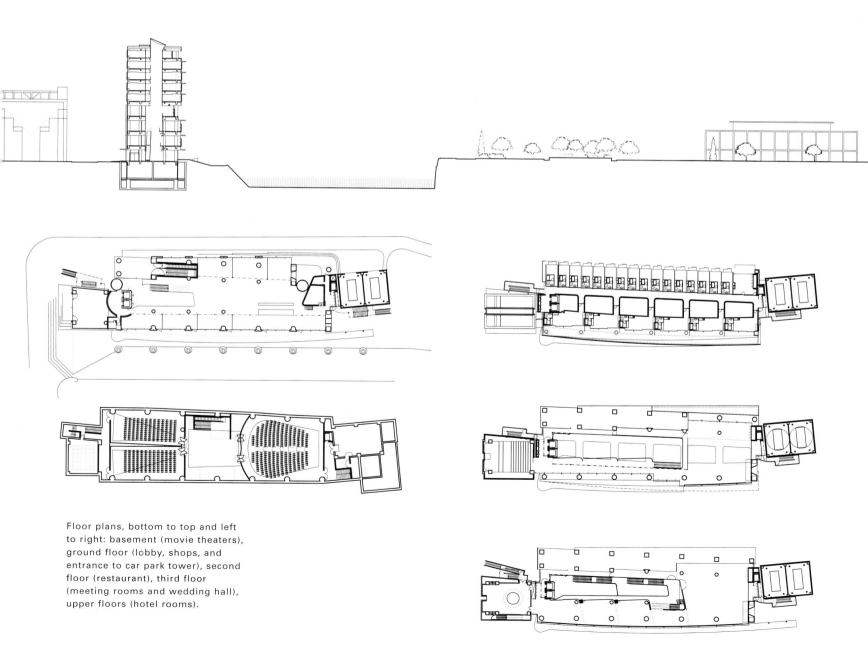

Floor plans, bottom to top and left to right: basement (movie theaters), ground floor (lobby, shops, and entrance to car park tower), second floor (restaurant), third floor (meeting rooms and wedding hall), upper floors (hotel rooms).

spin

***Revolving panoramic hall of the Oriental Pearl Tower.
Shanghai (1994-1995)***

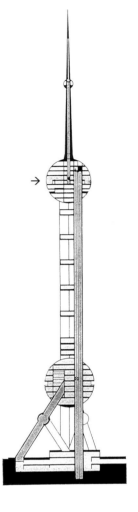

↑ The Oriental Pearl Tower in the skyline of Shanghai's Pu Dong area.
Right, cross section showing Spin's location within the tower.

→ The project consists of two floors within the sphere which crowns the Oriental Pearl Tower in Shanghai, China. Rising up to 460 meters, this is the highest communication tower in Asia and the third highest in the world – a tremendously important symbol for the people of Shanghai and the expression of the city's role as a center for business and culture.

As the two floors are set within a large glass sphere, the circle becomes an ordering device and recurring design theme which incorporates the powerful presence of the structural shafts into a dual spatial organization: in the center, a solid and opaque core finished in black marble, and in the perimeter, an open fluid space characterized by colored surfaces and transparent materials.

Spin's lower floor, at 267 meters, contains a piano bar for intimate events and concerts, an open bar, stage and dance area, and a revolving restaurant in the double-height perimeter which looks out on panoramic views of the city. The upper floor contains a reception area from which the guests are taken to private karaoke rooms which overlook the revolving restaurant below. The central core around the elevators houses the kitchen, toilets, and storage areas.

While enjoying a moving view of the city, the guest is taken on a journey through the full color spectrum simultaneously applied in the color filters built into the ceiling's lighting and into the table lamps on the revolving platform. These lighting effects accentuate the experience of movement and provide a sense of location and orientation in this kinetic interior landscape.

Views of the revolving restaurant and the balcony space on the upper floor. The six circular sections of glass case that define the edge of the revolving area were built with recycled materials by a group of young international artists under the coordination of the graphic artist Peret and shipped from Barcelona to Shanghai.

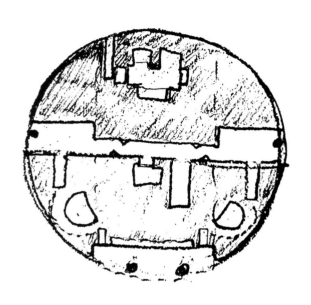

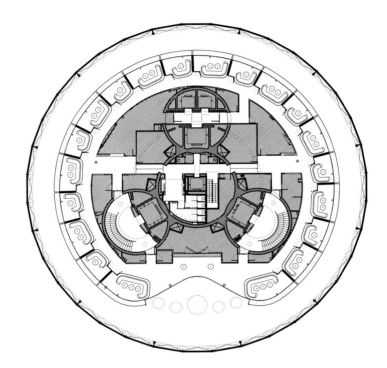

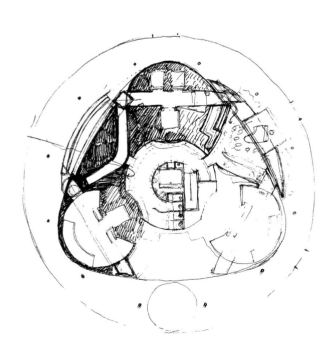

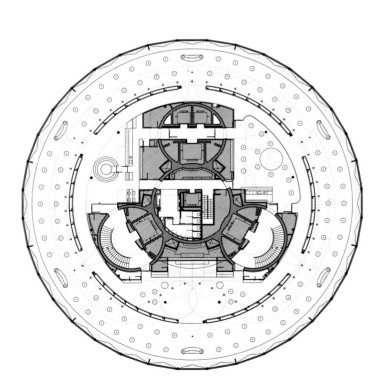

Top to bottom, left to right: early sketches of the massive structural core, floor plans, ceiling plans, and cross sections through the elevator shafts and through the central connecting corridor.

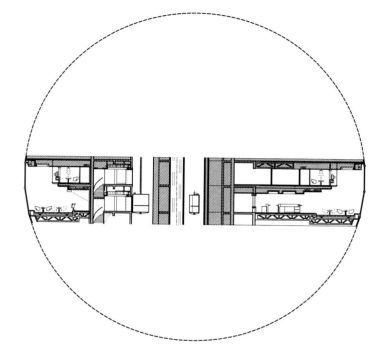

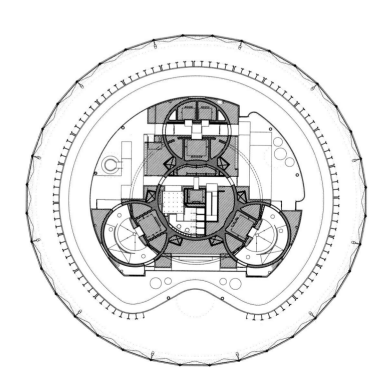

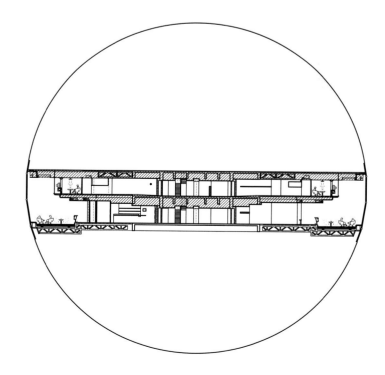

cosmo hall

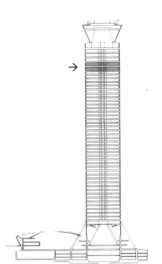

Ceremony halls and buffet restaurant in the World Trade Center building. Osaka (1994-1995)

→ Cosmo Hall is made up of conference rooms, spaces for Shinto and Christian religious ceremonies, and large banquet halls and a buffet restaurant occupying the 48th and 49th floors of the exclusive Osaka World Trade Center. As in the Spin project, the design is understood as a continuation of the containing architecture – here a standard highrise with a clear 1x2 modulation of the interior spaces and of the façades. In a composition which is reminiscent of traditional Japanese interiors, this modulation is applied to the new floors, ceilings and partitions, each made up of the repetition of a single specific element: a modulated carpet in two alternating colors, diffused light panels, and wall panels made of rusted iron. Only the two glass-enclosed ceremony halls on the upper floor stand as exceptions of the clear geometrical order of the layout. The service areas and logistic requirements of each space are densely grouped along each floor's central spine and define a compact structure enclosed by the new iron skin, whereas the restaurant and meeting halls are left as large open spaces surrounded by the glass façades and enjoying spectacular views of the city. The light, stackable Pila chair specifically designed for this space has since become one of the most widely used designs produced by the company.

↖Cross section showing the location of Cosmo Hall within Osaka's World Trade Center.
↑Views of a banquet/multipurpose room, a panel by Mariscal marking its entrance, and of the Eastern and Western ceremony halls. The project's modular composition is also applied to the glass façades, which frame the large views of the city.

The system of modular composition as applied in the design of the floors and ceilings of the two stories.
The plans on the right show the layout of the furnishings. Left, cross section.
The lower floor contains the main restaurant with a stage and a divisible multipurpose room on either side
of the central corridor and service spine.
The ceremony halls and another multipurpose room are located on the upper floor.

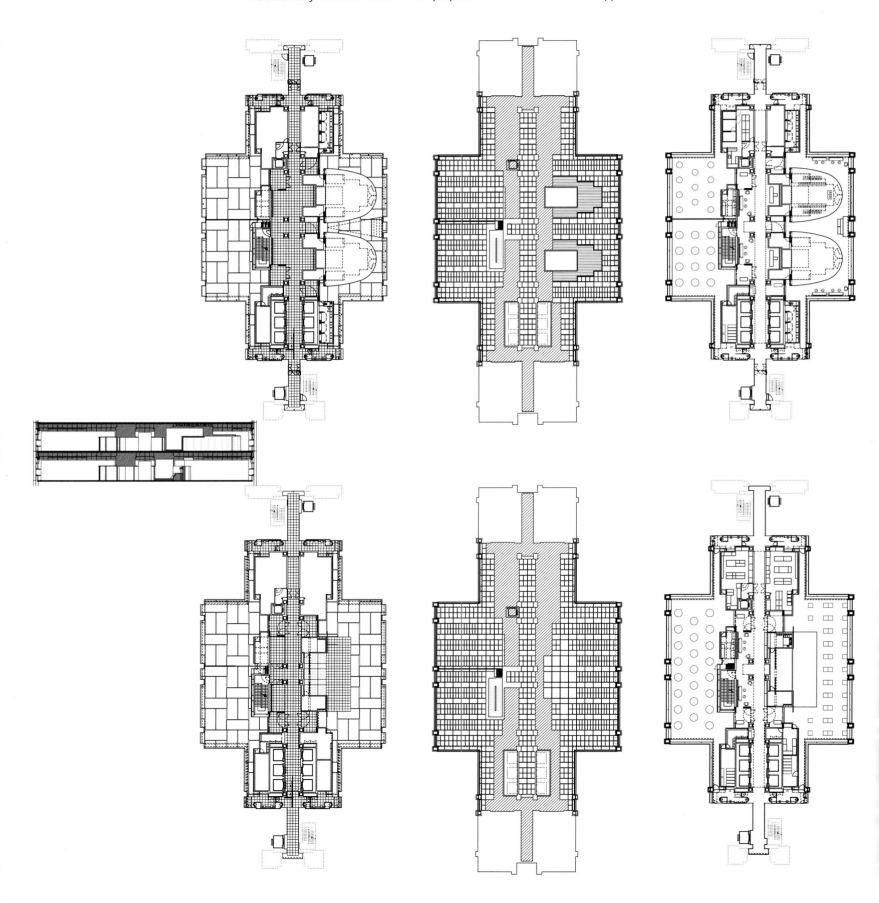

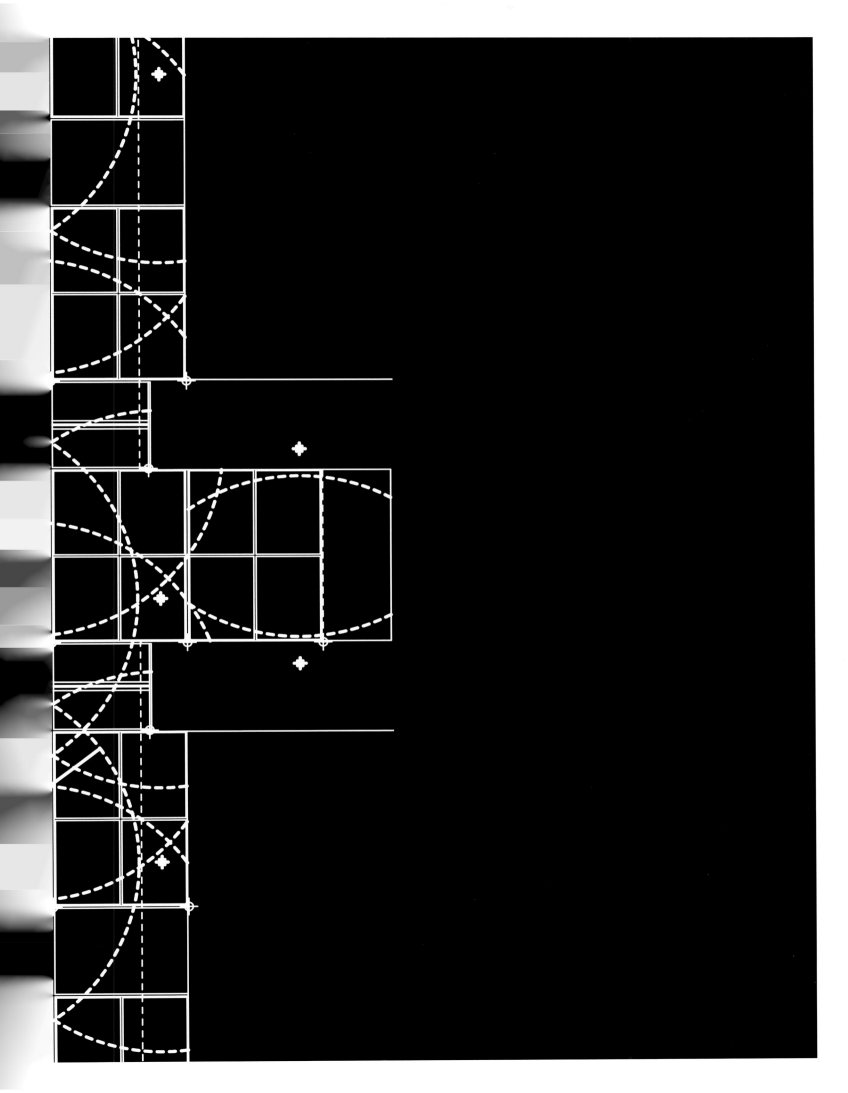

hung kuo building

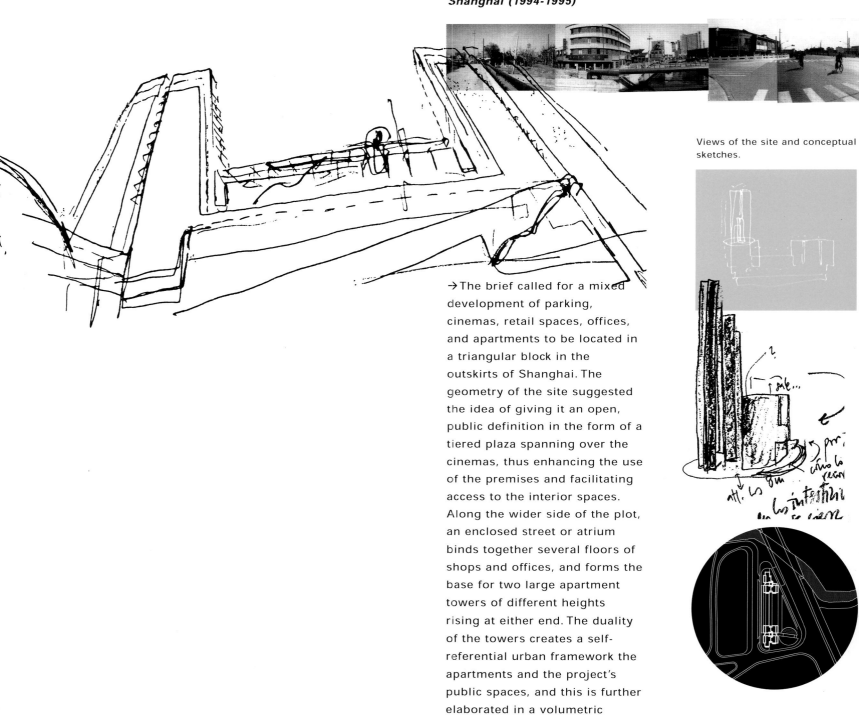

***Cinemas, shopping mall, and residential towers.
Shanghai (1994-1995)***

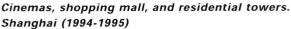

Views of the site and conceptual
sketches.

→The brief called for a mixed
development of parking,
cinemas, retail spaces, offices,
and apartments to be located in
a triangular block in the
outskirts of Shanghai. The
geometry of the site suggested
the idea of giving it an open,
public definition in the form of a
tiered plaza spanning over the
cinemas, thus enhancing the use
of the premises and facilitating
access to the interior spaces.
Along the wider side of the plot,
an enclosed street or atrium
binds together several floors of
shops and offices, and forms the
base for two large apartment
towers of different heights
rising at either end. The duality
of the towers creates a self-
referential urban framework the
apartments and the project's
public spaces, and this is further
elaborated in a volumetric
composition defined by an
alternating system of solid and
open bands which stress the
building's slender vertical
proportions.

↑Site plan.
→The model shows the
entrance pavilion and its glass
atrium in the foreground.
This structure serves as the
connecting core of the complex.

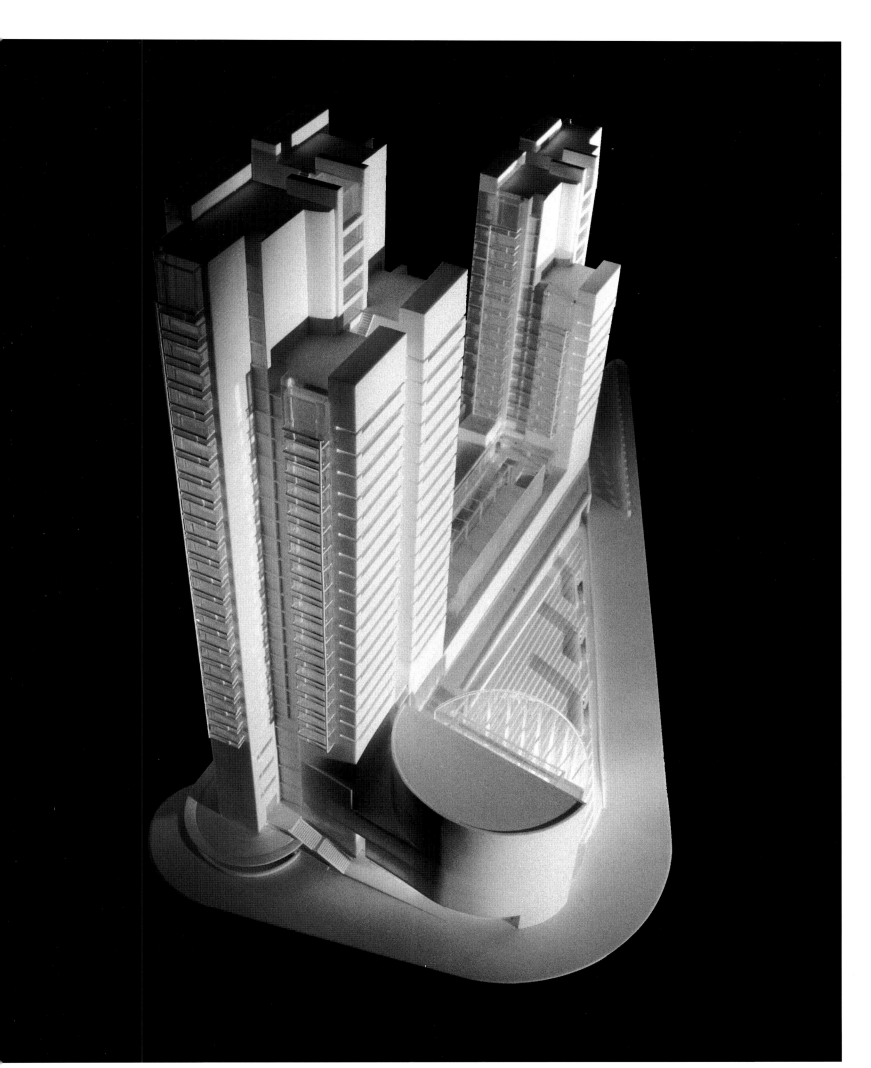

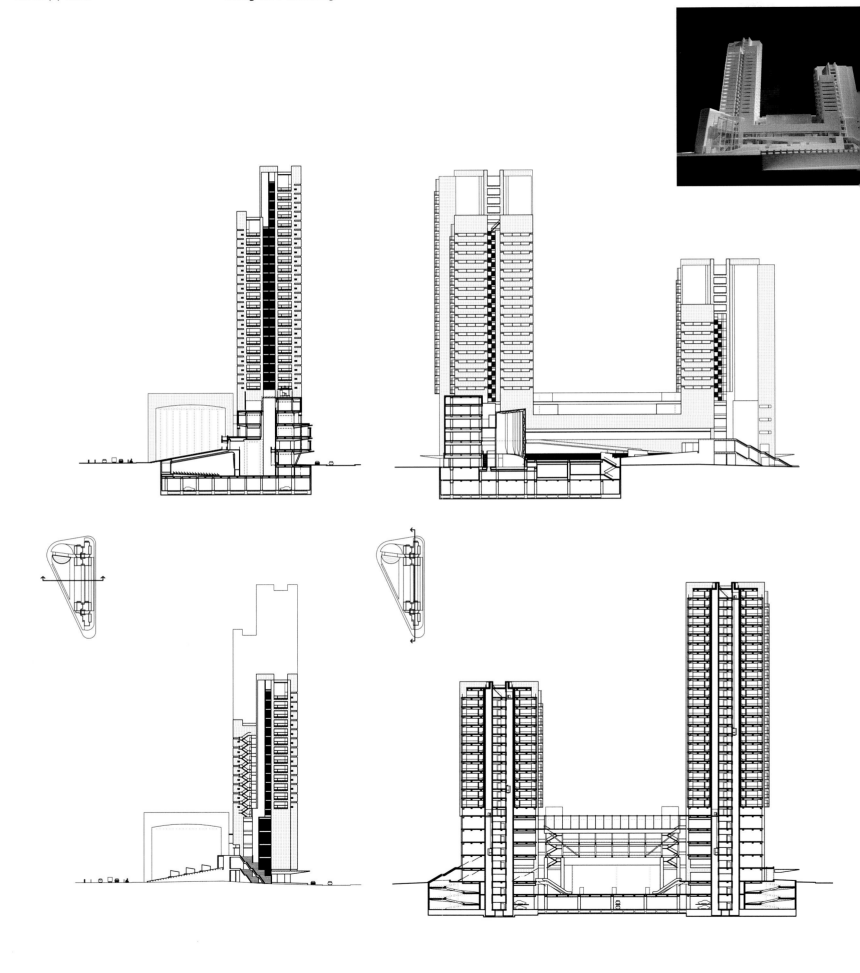

←Sections and elevations of the towers. The steel bridge between them defines the hall of the cinemas and connects the retail spaces.
↓The floor plans organized from bottom to top and left to right show the gradual change of functions: cinemas, tiered plaza,
retail spaces and offices, apartment towers.

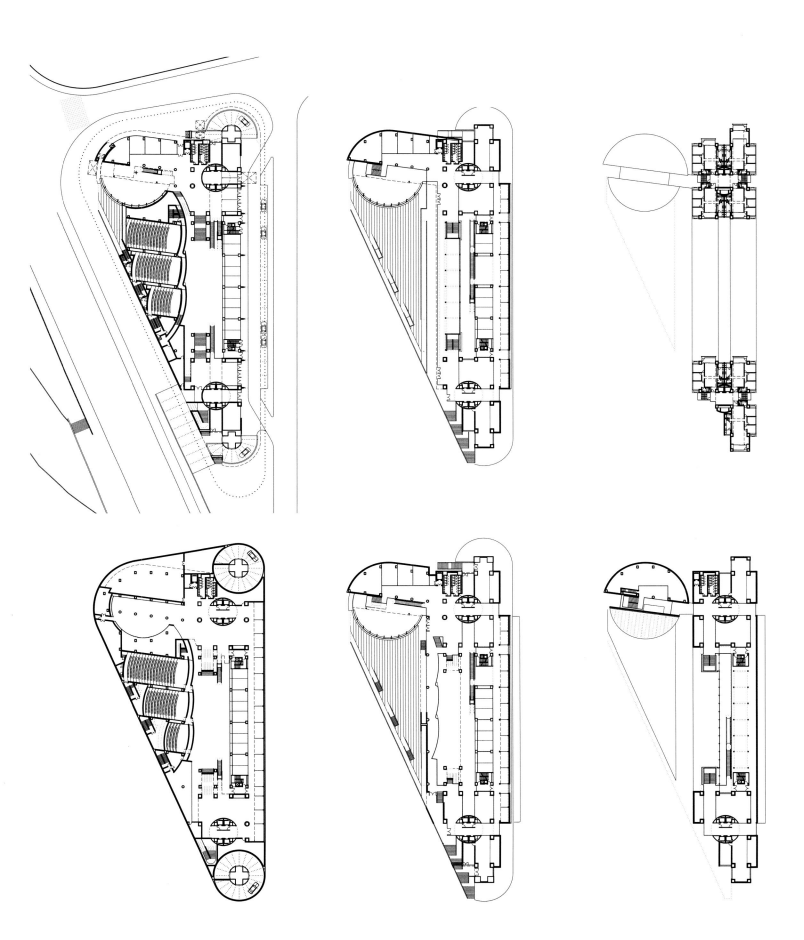

frankfurt and the german connection

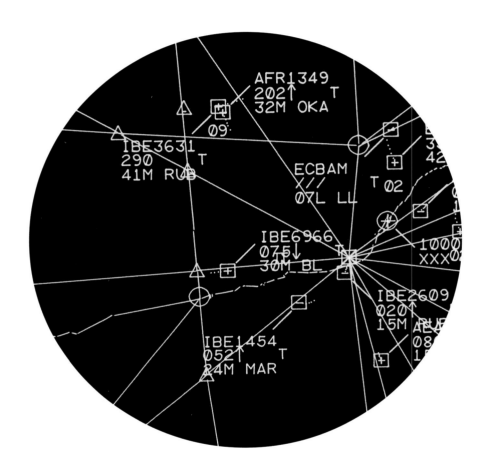

→In-tricate: from the Latin *tricae*: small detail, fragment, scrap. Intricate: dwelling on detail, attending to what is diverse, getting involved.

The theoreticians of the modern aesthetic, such as Burke, introduced the notion of *intricacy* to characterize the aesthetic effect of complexity as both the experience of an increase in stimuli and temptation as well as the endeavour to advance in or incorporate the manifold.

There is an architecture of intricacy, not just in landscaping, which is the genre in which the word had its heyday in the eighteenth century, but also in interior spaces, in passageways and connections.

On different occasions, Alfredo Arribas has professed an anti-minimalist faith – that is, he has declared his liking for the complex, inclusive, polymorphous.

In many cases his projects appear to begin with a simple idea, with a linear, elementary outline. But this initial outline, which he sometimes likes to produce in autographical drawings penned by an almost trembling hand, seems to be reconsidered in the design process as more and more detail is added and other, antagonistic movements are set up in opposition. Rather like the progress of the knight in chess: in contrast to the linear movement of the bishop or the pawn, the knight advances by moving first to one side, then to another. With no less belligerence, but leaping here and there.

In spite of differences in programme, or the fact that they are sometimes interventions in existing spaces and sometimes new, free-standing constructions, his buildings and projects in Germany always start out from a linear flow of movement and an envelope, be it circular, rectangular or elliptical. But the project grows with the proliferation of levels, with the artefacts of mechanical or pedestrian movement which indefatigably generate other rhythms, other spatial experiences, other paths and rough tracks.

The envelopes unfold, connections between inside and out lead to countless surprising perspectives.

In the most intensely worked stadium, in furnishings, partitions and objects, stability is exchanged for mobility, the sameness of materials is transmuted into a deliberate excess of unions, joints, of borrowed elements or entire quotations from the repertoires of time-honoured architectures (references to Aalto, Asplund, or Foster cannot escape anyone who devotes a little attention to his detail).

When Eugenio d'Ors, so fond of paradoxes, reached a certain point in his conceptual expositions, he would ask his audience: *Is that clear?* using the rhetorical question to confirm a long, analytical, deductive exposition. *Well if it is clear, let's make it confused again.* And back to the beginning.

Café and pavilion annex of the Schirn Kunsthalle. Frankfurt (1993-199

→ The renovation of the café of the monumental and austere Schirn Kunsthalle designed by Bangert, Jansen, Scholz and Schultes next to the red Frankfurt Cathedral was understood as an exercise in the continuation of what seemed to be an unfinished original space with few specific qualities beyond its connective use. Continuing the circular geometry of the floor plan, a new skin of pear wood which contrasts with the white stuccoed walls wraps the original structure and balconies of the galleries and multi-purpose rooms on the upper floors, and insulates them from the buzz of café life. Underneath, a long winding bar and a glass-enclosed kitchen continue this geometry and define the centrality of the room as well as the flows of people and the layout of the surrounding spaces: the restaurant – arranged along a bench that follows the curvature of the façade – and the open space that functions as a café during the day and a bar at night and opens onto the courtyard in the summer time.

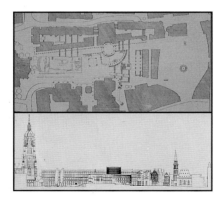

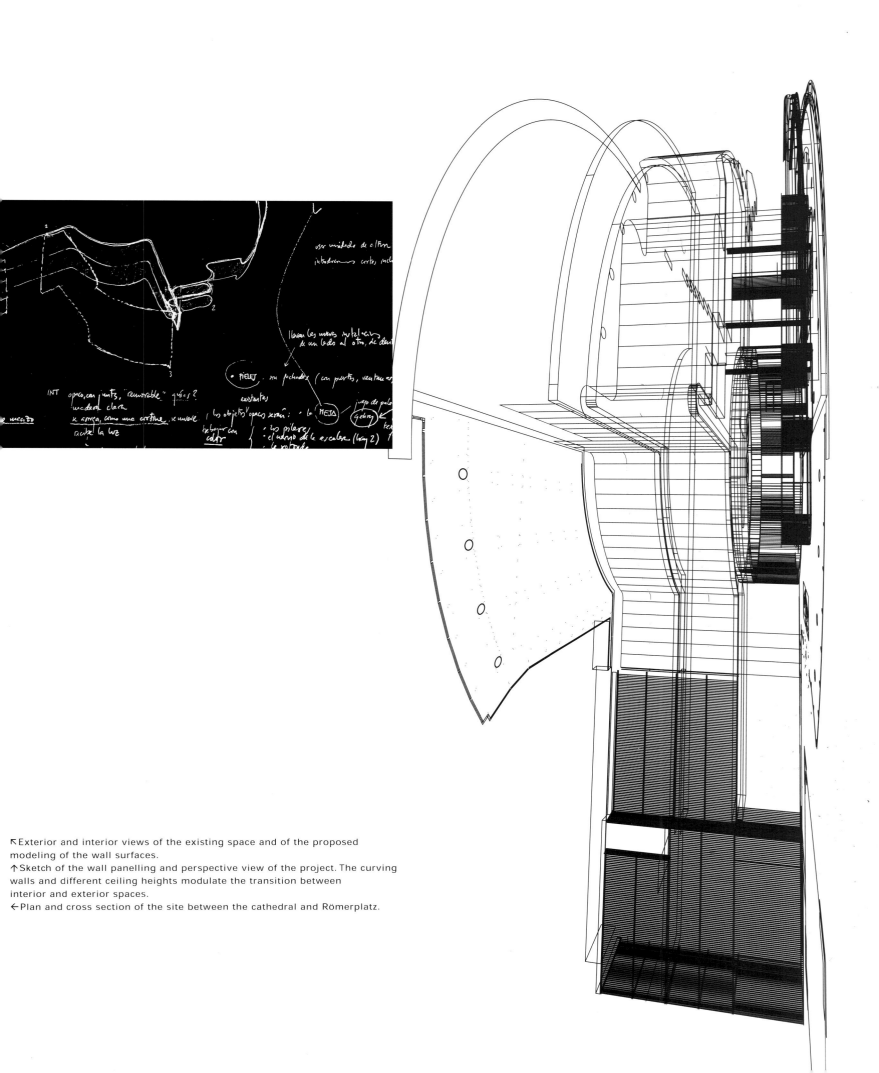

↖ Exterior and interior views of the existing space and of the proposed modeling of the wall surfaces.

↑ Sketch of the wall panelling and perspective view of the project. The curving walls and different ceiling heights modulate the transition between interior and exterior spaces.

← Plan and cross section of the site between the cathedral and Römerplatz.

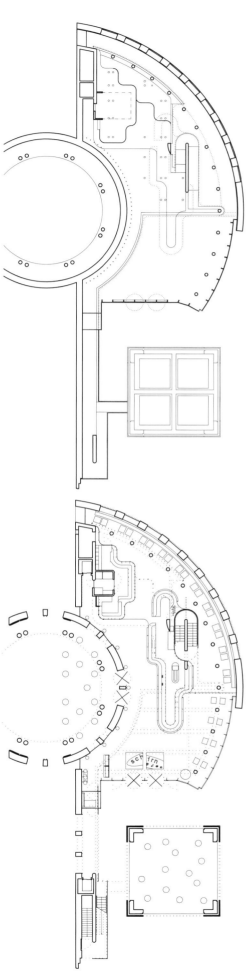

↗ Floor plan and ceiling plan. The square garden pavilion is shown below.

euronet/euromall

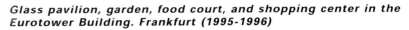

Glass pavilion, garden, food court, and shopping center in the Eurotower Building. Frankfurt (1995-1996)

→During the last decade, European cities have faced the need to transform the fabric of downtown areas by giving business areas made of autonomous, isolated office towers built in the 1960s and 70s a new culture of public space. In Frankfurt, the Euronet/Euromall – simultaneously a food court and a shopping mall – enhances the public use of the emblematic Eurotower building by establishing an increased interaction with its surroundings and bringing in new activities to this location. The project also increases pedestrian circulation across the central Willy Brandt Platz, and offers, by means of a new glass pavilion that redefines the building's base, a new gate to the giant tower. This pavilion, which partly modifies the original cross section of an underground parking space, creates a fluent transition between the public garden and the public interiors by allowing the unheeded flow of natural light.

Euronet/Euromall brings together different scales of intervention: urban and garden planning, architectural design and structural engineering in the new glass pavilion – where for the first time in Germany a new system of structural glazing for horizontal surfaces is applied – a new gastronomic concept, interior design, furniture design, and finally corporate identity and graphic design.

← View of the glass pavilion and square from the top of the Eurotower, and model of the project.
↙ The site plan shows the proximity of this project (bottom) to the Commerzbank Plaza building one block north.
↓ Sketches of the landscaping and park walkways.

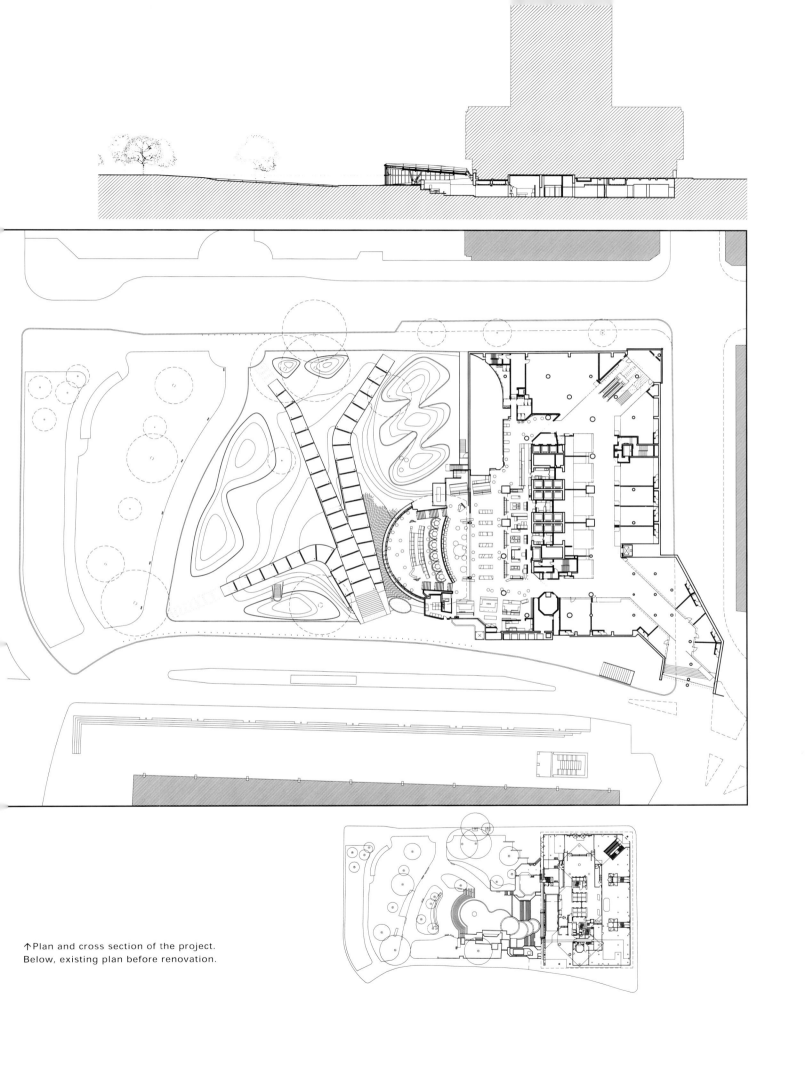

↑ Plan and cross section of the project.
Below, existing plan before renovation.

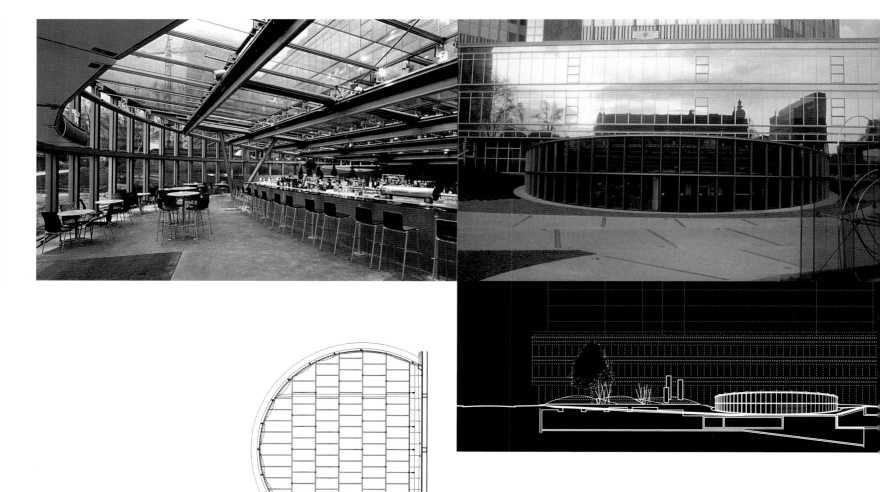

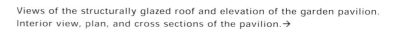

Views of the structurally glazed roof and elevation of the garden pavilion. Interior view, plan, and cross sections of the pavilion.→

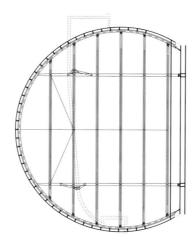

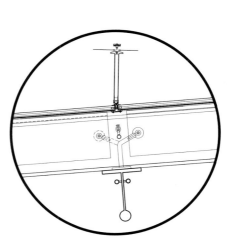

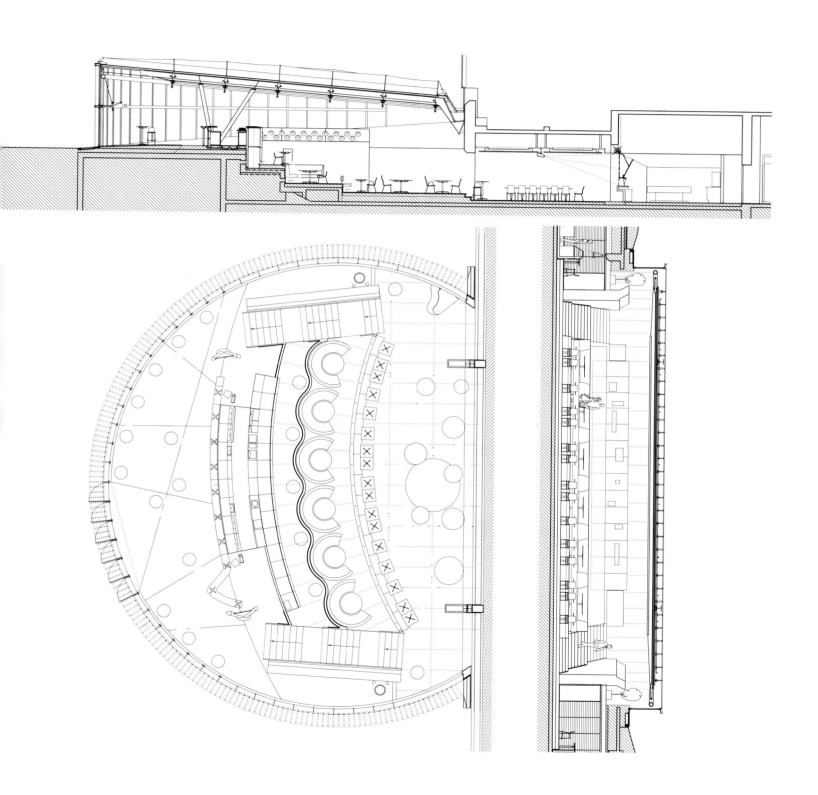

art hotel

Hotel renovation and extension. Wiesbaden (1995-1996)

↑Sketch of the building's new skin and corner tower. The preexisting volume is shown below.
Aerial photograph showing the location of the hotel in the city center. The site plan, model, and sketches show the relationship of the renovation project with the site.→

→ The city council of Wiesbaden, which owns this centrally located 1960s building, decided to hold a small competition to extend the existing hotel and to complement it with other activities. This project intends to reinforce the existing conference halls and the entertainment restaurant, and to include a new multifunctional space capable of accommodating theater representations or dinner parties.

Three major types of intervention are planned. At a town planning level, a new organization of vehicle access is suggested, which involves moving the main entrance to the opposite side of its existing location, and the reinforcement of the corner of the building as a marker, a sign of the activities it houses. A second intervention deals with the garden, which is fully incorporated into the building by means of a new transparent construction made of glass and steel which extends an existing curvilinear pavilion. Finally, the building is given a new glass skin allowing the passage of light, air and sunshine, and which extend the rooms into a sort of sunroom space overlooking the garden.

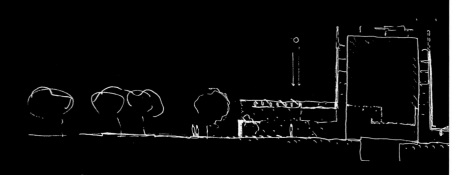

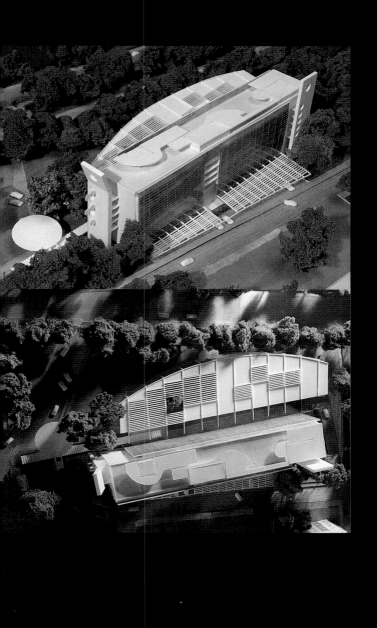

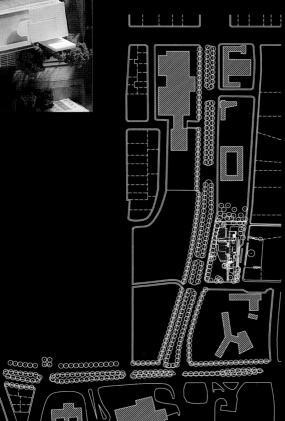

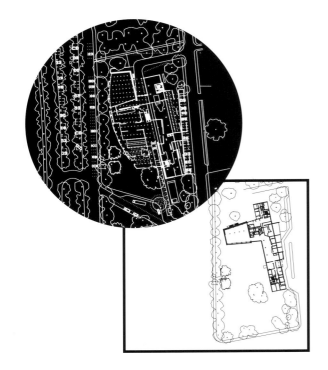

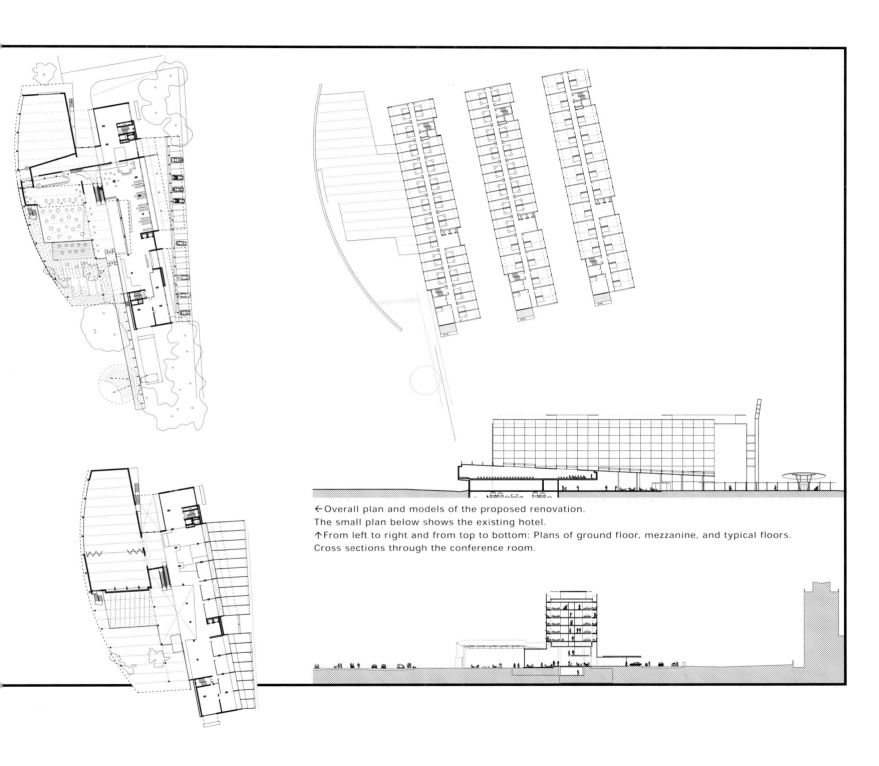

←Overall plan and models of the proposed renovation.
The small plan below shows the existing hotel.
↑From left to right and from top to bottom: Plans of ground floor, mezzanine, and typical floors.
Cross sections through the conference room.

fun factory

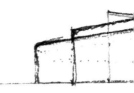

Entertainment and sports park. Leipzig (1995-1996)

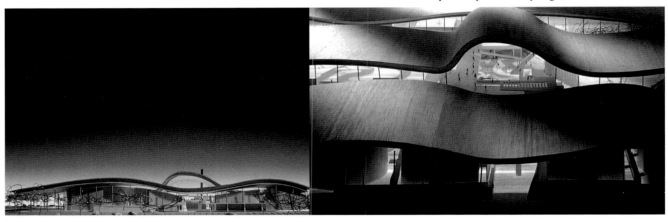

→ This project, designed for the periphery of Leipzig, lacks a concrete site and was conceived as being subject to constant evolution. The Fun Factory is a leisure center which houses games and sports areas, cinemas and a disco within containers defined by wide bays, simple construction techniques, and a great deal of flexibility. These activities occupy six volumes which are connected at two levels by a continuous concrete floor slab. The project originally started out from a simple formal proposal in response to a commission to design a logistic park, however, as the functional program evolved, the spatial containers were gradually modeled in plan and cross section to adapt to the different activities. As a result of these programmatic requirements, an expressive undulating roof landscape manifests the varying activities carried out inside and responds directly to the emergence of ramps or other elements above the base plane.

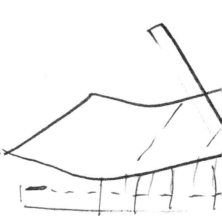

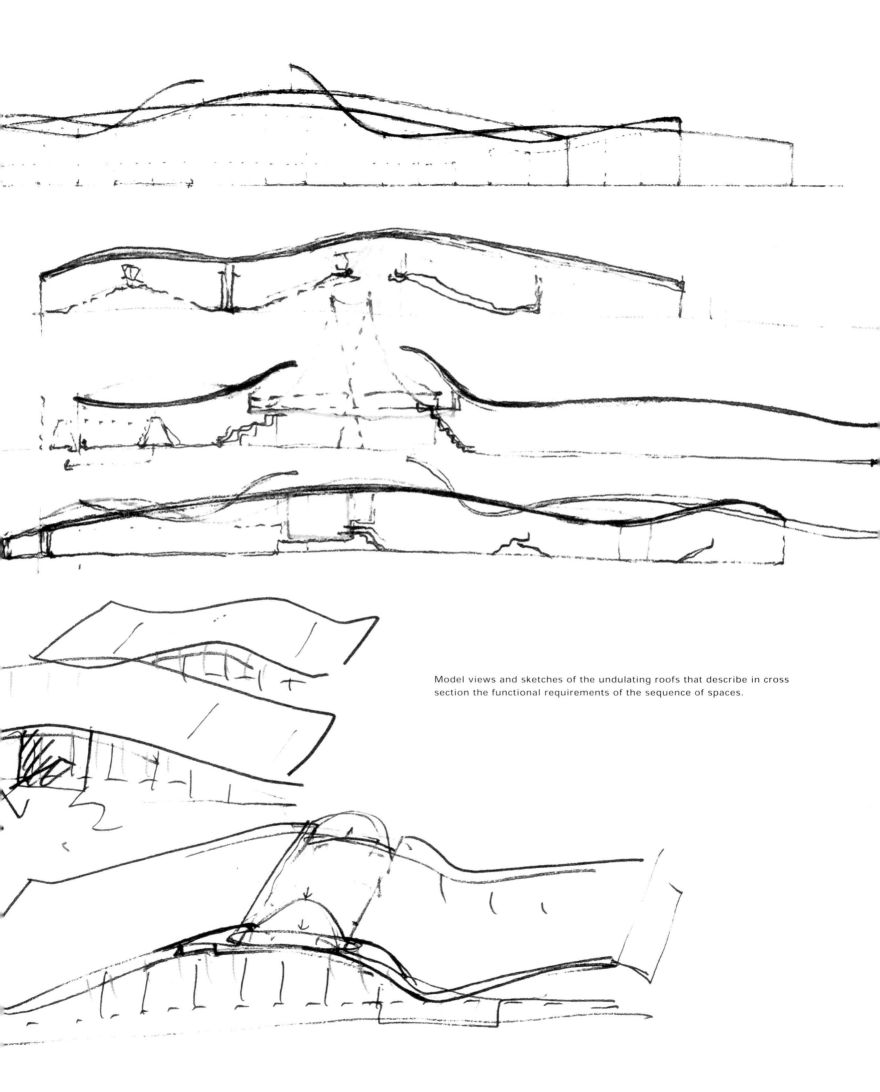

Model views and sketches of the undulating roofs that describe in cross section the functional requirements of the sequence of spaces.

←Study model of the preliminary proposal for a multipurpose logistic park.
→Views of the presentation model and plan.

MULTIPLEXKINO

MULTIPLEXKINO

DISCO

MULTIFUNKTIONSHALLE
INDOOR SKATING

INDOOR KART

BILLARD

STREETBALL

AEROBIC

FITNESS
MEETING

BOWLING

BADMINTON

SQUASH

SUPERBOWL

FAST FOOD

FITNESS

TICKETS

KINO FOYER

DISCO

AMERICAN BAR

HOCKENHEIM FOYER

KIOSK

WERKSTATT

TECHNIK

COCKTAIL BAR

RESTAURANT

TRIBÜNE

INFOBÖRSE

FERRARI SHOP

SHOP

UMKLEIDE

SAUNA

MASSAGE

INFO

ICH RECHTSANWALT

ERNÄHRUNGS-
BERATUNG

ARZT

DRIVE IN

commerzbank plaza

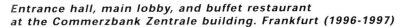

Entrance hall, main lobby, and buffet restaurant at the Commerzbank Zentrale building. Frankfurt (1996-1997)

→ The Plaza is a new public indoor space incorporated in the Commerzbank Zentrale building, the highest skyscraper in Frankfurt. As a transitional space between the city center and the bank offices, it has been simultaneously conceived as a café and a cultural space that houses temporary art exhibitions and is used as the Commerzbank staff dining area, with as many as 1200 customers per day served within 2 to 3 hours. Following the original architectural language of this project by Foster Associates, the space has been divided in two areas by means of a curved row of revolving, propeller-like panels that allow for a changing layout of the space at different times. All sorts of facilities, as kitchens, toilets, dish belt, etc. are located in the lowest and irregular area behind these panels. Cool materials, as iron, stainless steel or epoxy concrete, are used in the service

areas, whereas wood, carpets and glass are used in the main space. In order to avoid the proliferation of chairs and tables stranded after use in such a space, the possibilities of having lunch vary from a free-flow, self-service cafeteria to a formal restaurant, allowing for four different sitting positions. "Der Wurm," a long wooden platform which folds and bends to create an ensemble of long wooden benches, is the strongest design intervention. Conceived as an enormous wooden sculpture when it is not used, this element allows for 200 customers to be seated at the same time. Hidden by this structure are ten long sliding tables that can be extended to seat 100 additional customers at peak times. The Plaza's name and graphic image were created in collaboration with the visual poet Joan Brossa.

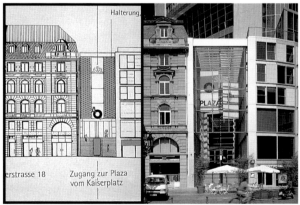

↑ View from the main lobby of the building. The Plaza, which can also be accessed from the street, defines the extended public base of the Commerzbank Zentrale building.
← Site plan showing the Plaza's proximity to Euronet/Euromall.
↓ Plan of the building's ground floor → Façade of street access and visual poem.

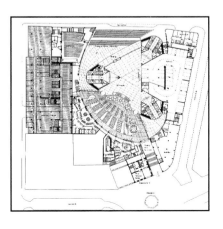

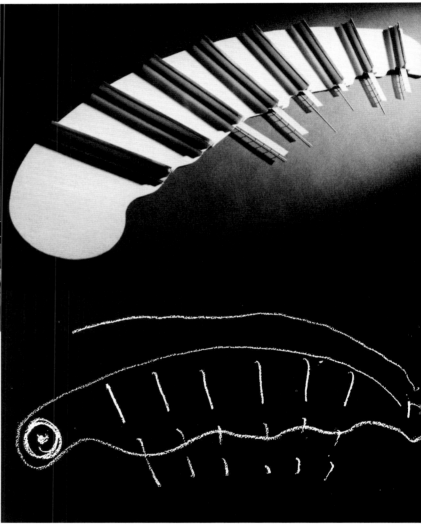

Sketch, study model, and view of "Der Wurm" (the worm).

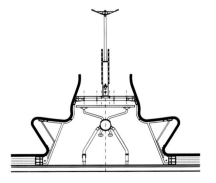

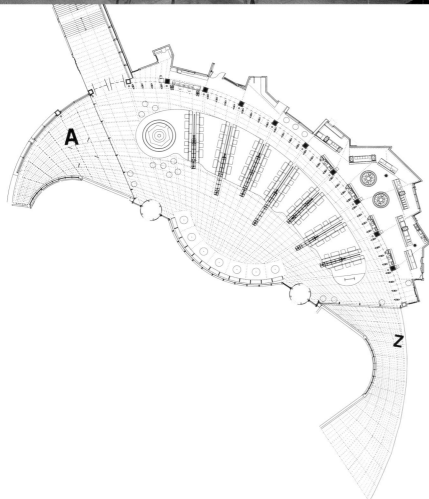

↙Floor plan and ceiling plan showing the location of the kitchens and cloakrooms in the spaces that define the irregular perimeter.
↓The rotating panels that divide these service areas from the restaurant.

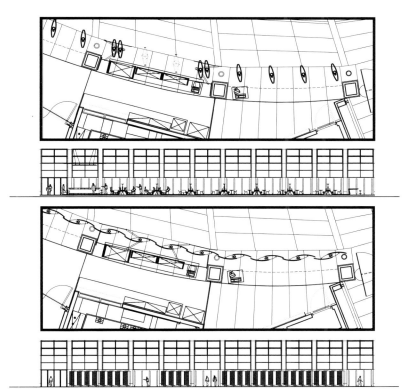

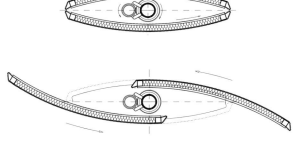

domestic

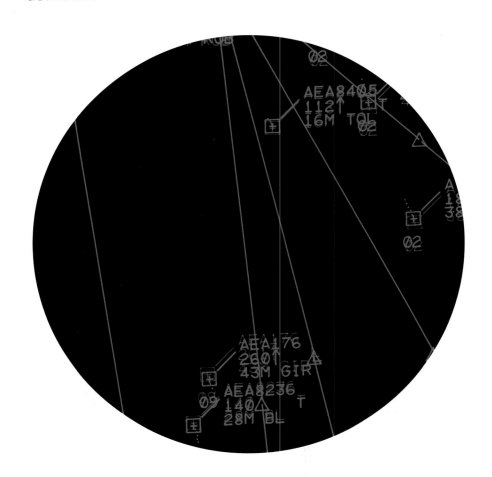

→The two *Domestic Exercises* included in chapter four of this book are extremely interesting. Both the house on Teodoro Roviralta Street and the Meyer-Paulus houses clearly confirm the colonizing intent which marks most of Alfredo Arribas' projects.

Understanding architecture as colonization means taking up a position halfway between the production of architecture as a pure, autonomous object and the production of architecture as a pure insertion in an existing context.

To colonize means to occupy a territory. Sometimes supposedly *virgin, natural,* untouched by human hands.

But colonising also – in most cases – means occupying by force, imposing a new regime or a different order on the occupied place. However, in both cases colonization measures itself against the occupied territory and establishes its new order by comparing itself with its predecessor in such a way that colonization becomes a combination of the force of imposition and the acumen of grafting.

A considerable number of Alfredo Arribas' works, not just the domestic ones, are marked by this colonizing attitude. More specifically, many of them come to the place to settle down and create a new order.

The Meyer house and the Paulus house appear to grow on a hill, more than anything like geometries, like the colonizing gestures of a topography that has gained strength with the intervention. A nervous dynamism running in every direction is the shaft that defines the resulting tension in each of the buildings and in the relationship between them and the territory. Multiplied directions, slidings, open and arborescent geometries are the support for an active, almost aggressive occupation of the place and landscape.

Yet the projects for work on existing buildings are no less colonizing. The intervention Arribas proposes in two conventional, early twentieth-century houses, with a view to turning them into a single building for a house-cum-study, is no less forceful in its intent to occupy, though in this case it is not a landscape but a context which has already been established by the existing architecture.

The act of colonizing, in the Medinaceli and Sanson buildings or in Lisbon's Chiado and many other renovations and interiors carried out or designed by Alfredo Arribas, is always a confrontation: taking on board certain references to produce a new system of spaces.

Like Duchamp's *objet trouvé,* the houses on Teodoro Roviralta are incorporated like a residue, like a memory, into a new organization and a system of totally different spaces and passages. The existing architectural heritage facing the architect was deliberately turned into something else, into other values whose dominance of the *trouvé* never leaves the slightest room for doubt.

teodoro roviralta

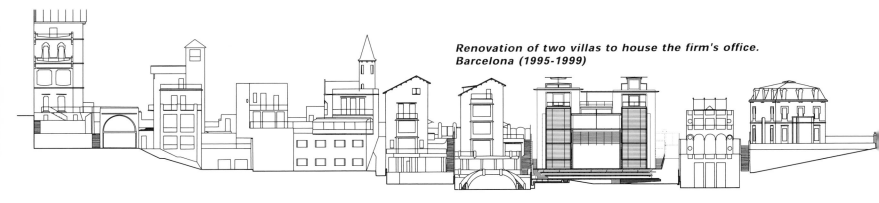

**Renovation of two villas to house the firm's office.
Barcelona (1995-1999)**

Site plan and photograph of the garden
side of the street's row of houses.
The project renovates and extends
towards the garden the first two
houses on the right, as shown in the
elevation and the model views.

→ The project is located on a
steep site at the foot of the hills
surrounding Barcelona, in one
of the rare streets still
characterized by an abundance
of villas from the turn of the
century. Slowly developed in the
course of six years it consists of
two twin houses which are
grouped and extended – in
clear opposition to the existing
architecture – by means of
transparent volumes made of an
exposed steel structure and
glass façades. The floors of the
old houses have been hollowed
and become simple containers
integrated by the unifying
addition in a new elongated and
flowing spatial configuration
that defines a new front for the
garden. The continuity of the
spaces is also enhanced by the
simple detailing and
constructional grammar of the
structure, the façades, and the
moving partitions. Between the
two houses on the street side, a
system of staircases leading to
the different studios revolves
around a central glass elevator
shaft. The cross section with
street and garden access at
different levels allows for the
creation of independent
accesses to the different studios
and workshops and for an open
relationship between interior

and exterior spaces. The unified
building is roofed with light and
mobile sun-shading structures
which offer a new interpretation
of the symmetrical profile of the
former houses.

View from the street of the two houses and of the
intermediate system of independent accesses revolving around the glass lift.
↓Street elevation.

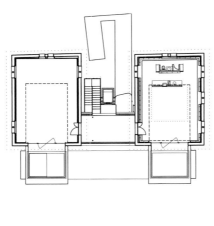

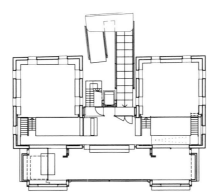

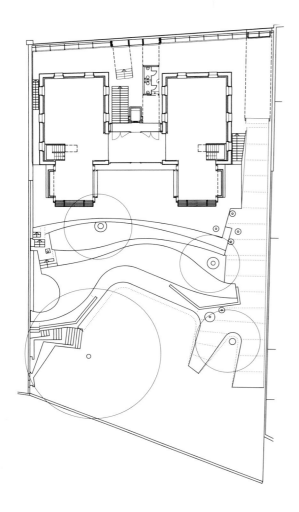

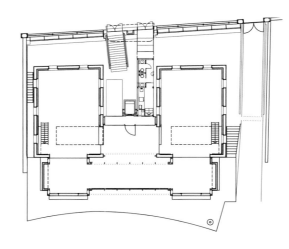

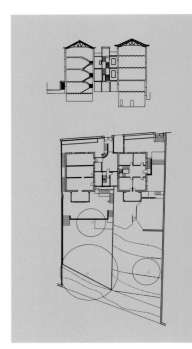

Plan and cross section before renovation.
← Floor plans. Counterclockwise from left: basement -1 (garden), ground floor, first floor (entrance), second floor.
↙ Below, perpendicular cross sections through the center of the intermediate connecting volumes.

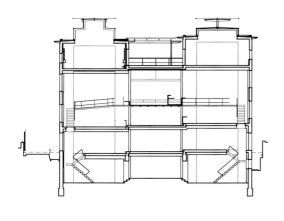

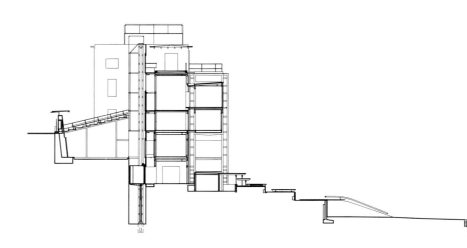

Homes for two families. La Zagaleta, Málaga (1996-1998)

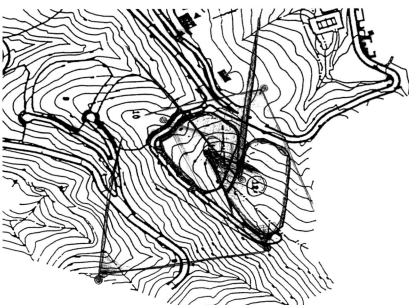

Site plan with road access and view
from the upper right corner of the
plan, looking south-east towards the
hill on which the houses are designed.

→These two neighboring houses
were to be built on a rugged
piece of land with spectacular
views of the southern
Mediterranean coast of Spain
reaching down to Gibraltar. In
response to the natural qualities
of this setting, the large
required built areas are
functionally broken up into a
sequence of volumes closely
related to the ground surface
and the views.

The different slopes and relative
positions of the neighboring
sites as well as a different
degree of participation from the
clients lead the design
processes of the
programmatically similar houses
into two different directions.
Since the early sketches the plan
of the Meyer house, located on
the steep mountainside, has zig-
zagged downwards in a
continuous, centrifugal
movement that begins in the
garage and ends in the
bedrooms and seeks to extend
the domestic activities into the
surroundings. An inclined roof
plane unifies this fragmented
volumetric organization and
refers the house to the original

topography of the site.

The plan of the Paulus house, to
be built on the hilltop is
conditioned by the need to
respond to the traditional
typology of the patio house,
with its inward views and
centripetal organization of the
plan. The house is divided into
two elementary volumes which
are grouped in a V-shaped plan
and covered by an inverted
pitched roof. The semi-enclosed
courtyard in the form of an
impluvium relates the interior
spaces and frames the views of
the distant landscape.

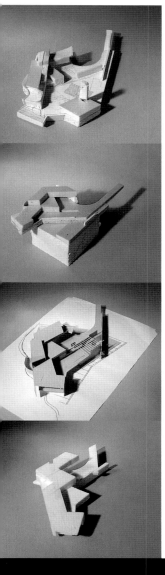

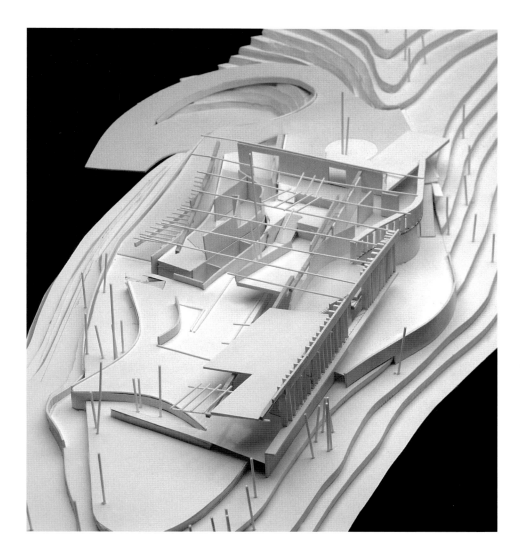

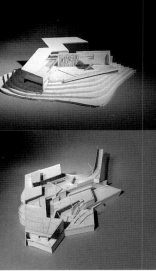

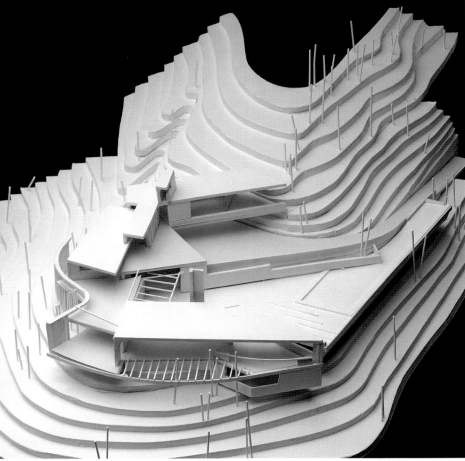

Working models of the
Meyer house (left) and
of the Paulus house
without its roof.

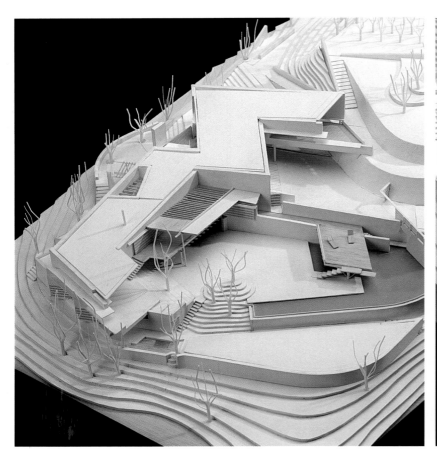

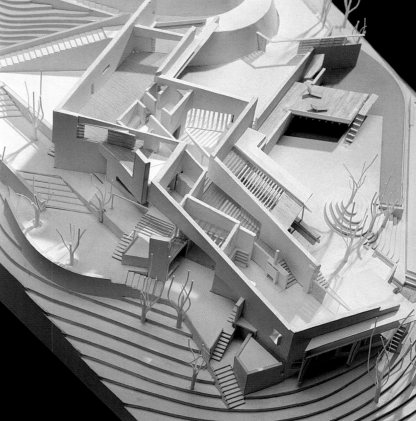

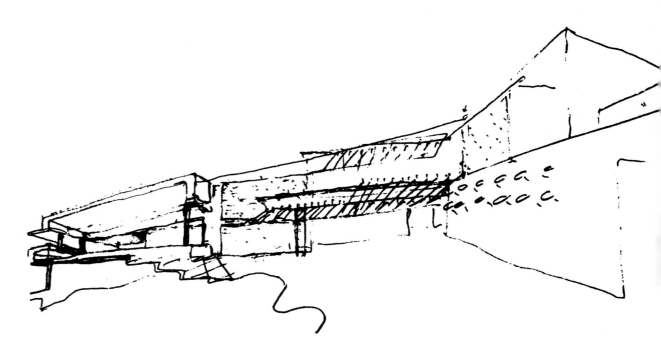

The Meyer house. Views of the model without and with the roof plane and sketch from the courtyard terrace. The building bridges this exterior space to allow through views of the landscape.

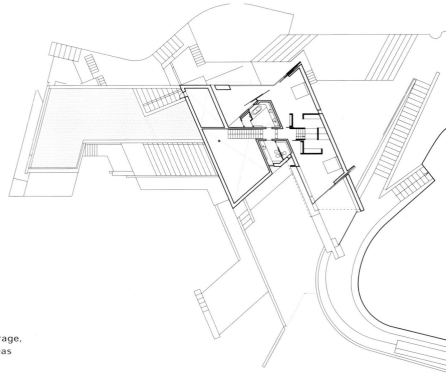

Floor plans, clockwise from top: upper floor (main bedrooms), middle floor (garage, reception hall, kitchen, dining and living rooms), and lower floor (children's areas and bedrooms).
Sections and elevations.→

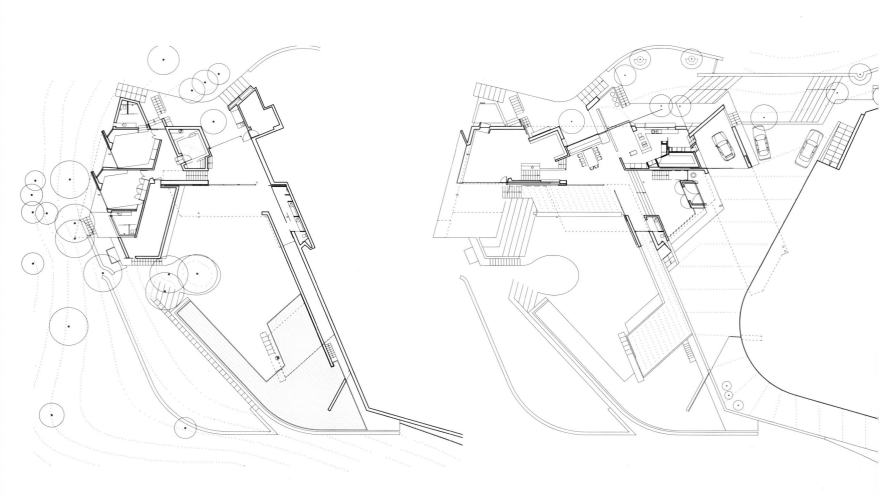

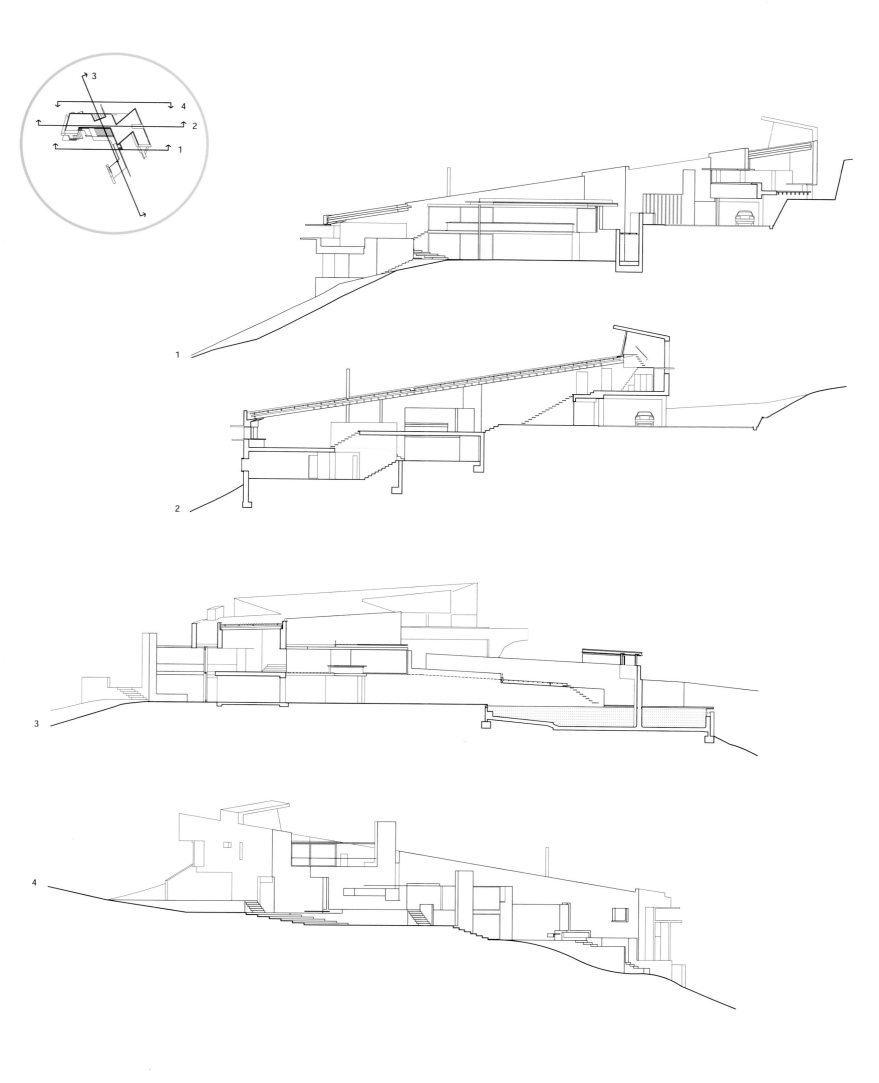

1

2

3

4

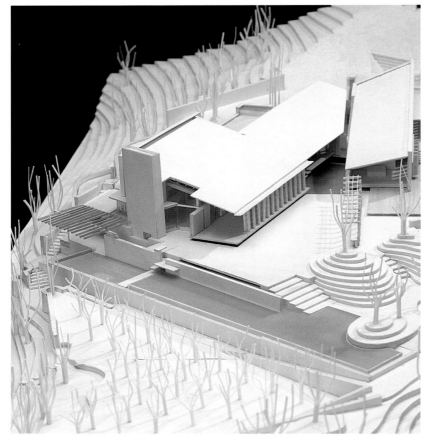

The Paulus house. Views of the model with and without the roof plane and sketches of the patio concept.

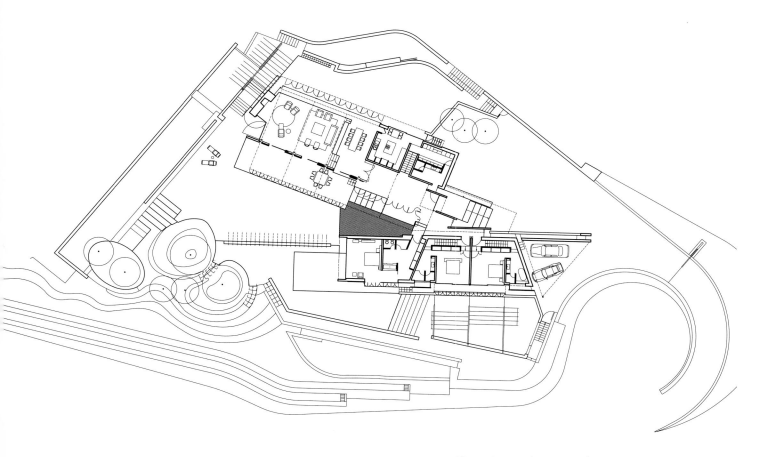

Floor plans and cross sections.
The upper floor is divided in the common living wing and the bedroom
wing for the clients and their children. The lower floor contains a
library-study also used as a family room near the swimming pool and
the grandchildren's bedrooms.

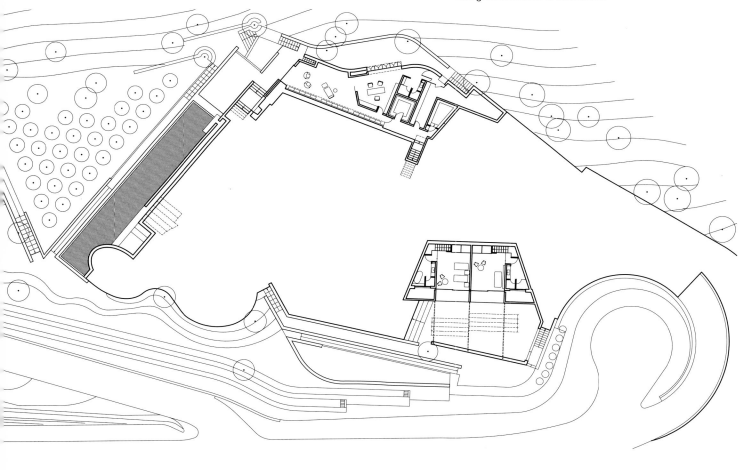

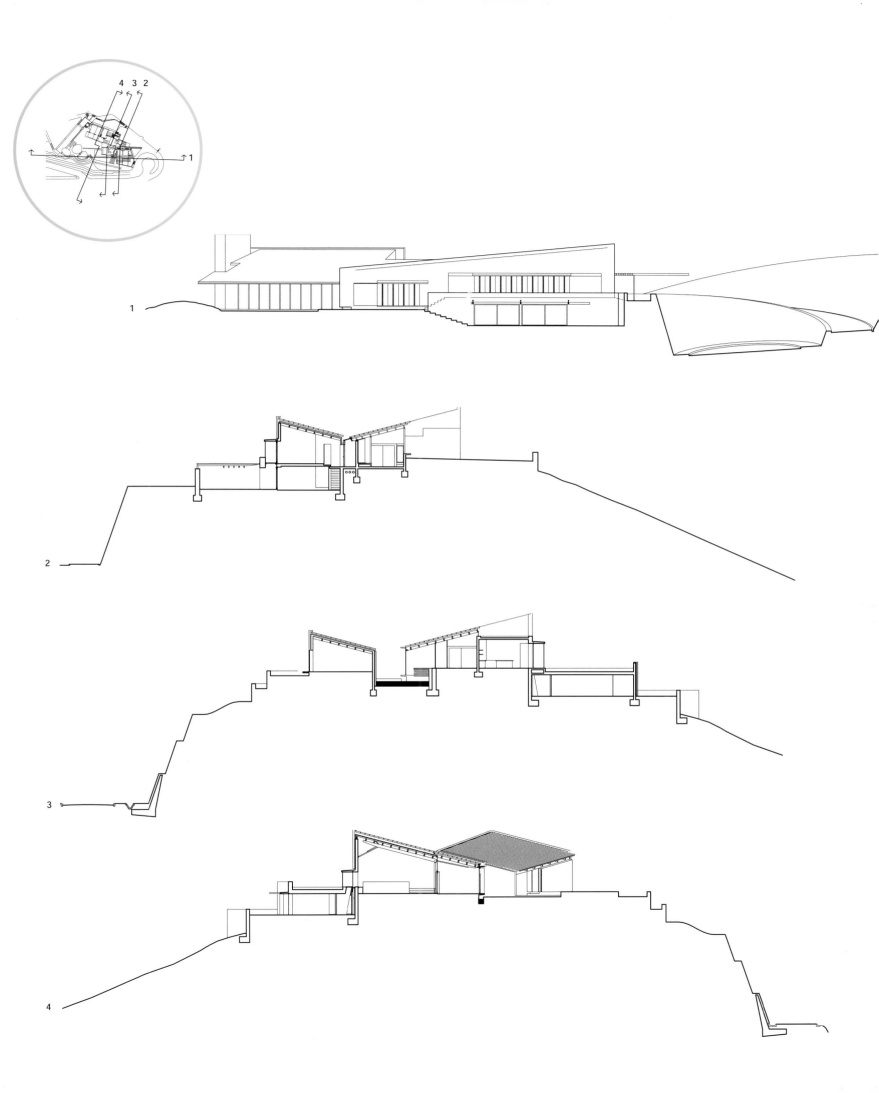

1

2

3

4

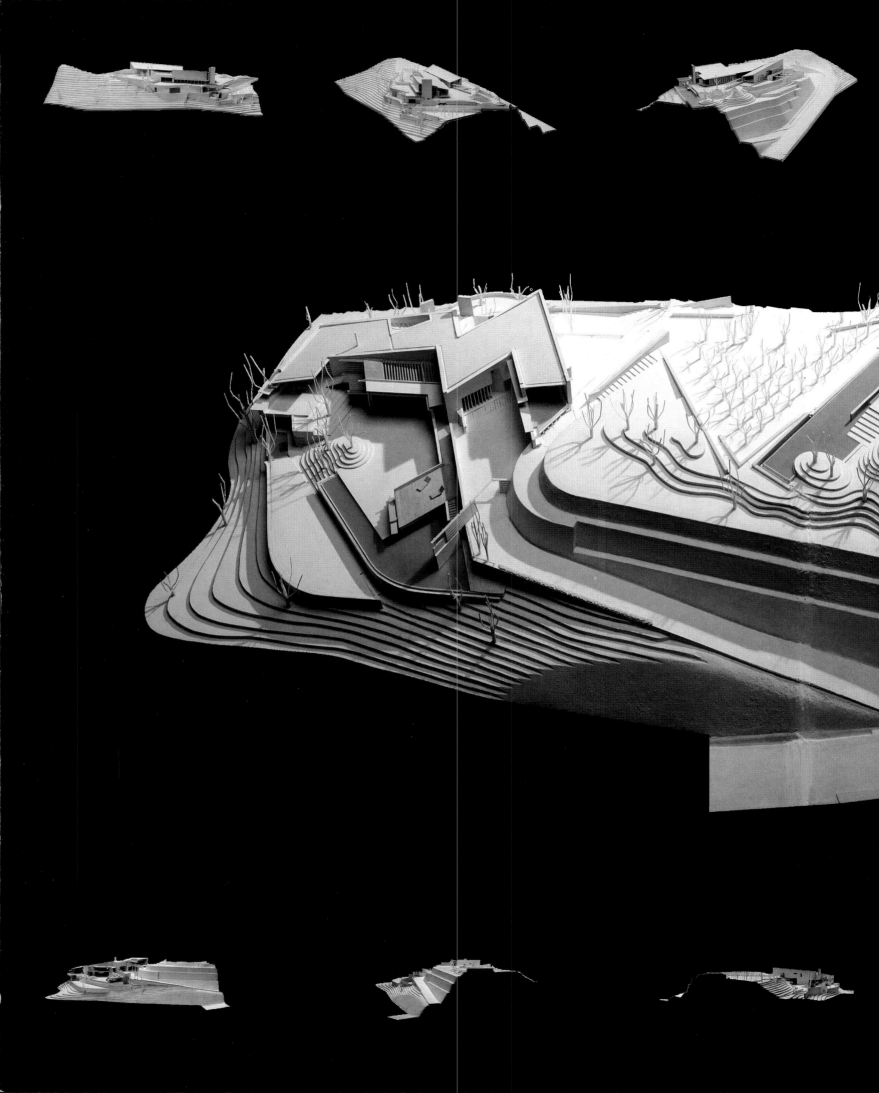

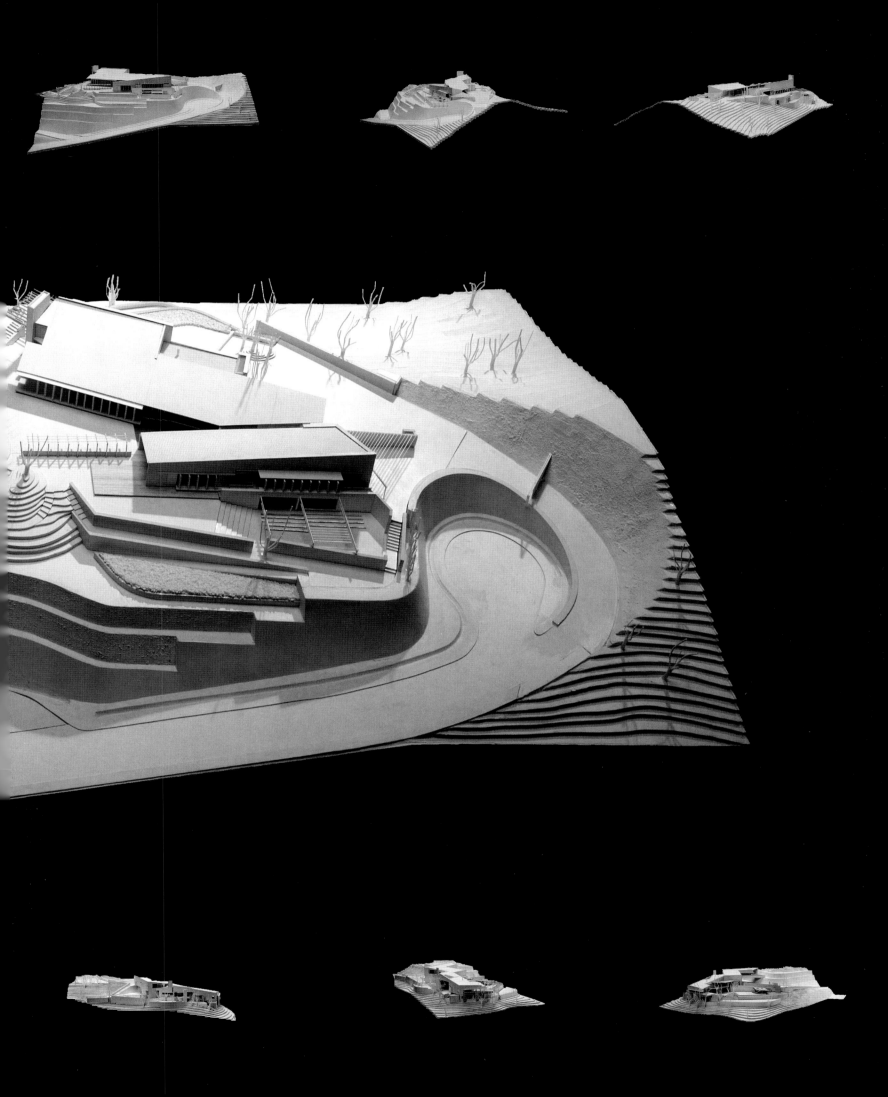

europa europa

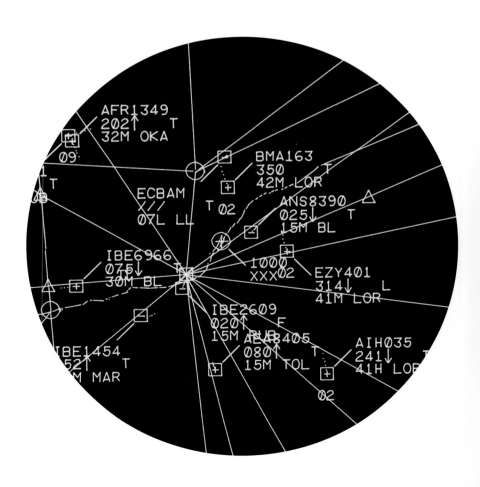

→In my introductory text I referred to the distance that separates the position of Reyner Banham and the attitude implied by Alfredo Arribas' body of work. Banham retrieves a degree of the orthodoxy of modernity, brought up to date, which provided the ideological basis for *high-tech* architecture. The forms of architecture covered by this term are based on a fascination with the machine as the most fitting expression of modern rationality and efficiency.

The mechanical metaphor also has a hand in Alfredo Arribas' works: interlinked devices and energy flows seem to feed the movement of buildings and the functioning of their many appliances. But the mechanical reference does not stem from either Schlemmer or Le Corbusier; it is reminiscent of the celibate, unproductive machines which Marcel Duchamp came up with for his project, *Le Grand Verre*. Fluid energies, throbs of desire, informal air currents, aberrant gazes and labyrinthine deviations are the true driving forces of machines which, rather than yielding productive efficiency, seem to invite festive extravagance, waste of resources and endless proliferation in the style of Bataille's anti-economy. Anyone who looks at the *inventions* and machines which constantly appear in our architect's increasingly liberated projects and takes them seriously, literally, is bound to be misled. Escalators, rotating platforms, vehicular and pedestrian junctions, active connections between different parts of a whole, an escalation of stimuli to attract the delirious, erratic visitor.

It is no coincidence that quite a few of the projects appearing in this chapter have a marked relationship with the theme-park effect dominating the leisure activities on offer in our late-capitalist societies. There is no apparent distinction between a showroom for a specific product and other places expressly conceived as museums or theme parks, all of them are dominated by a logic which bears the stamp of the same architectural approach.

The theme-park effect is surely one of the great challenges facing contemporary architecture. The construction of places which propose other places with the utmost persuasive ability but not without introducing individual choice. Selection as a purely subjective decision: these are the keys to any such process of "Disneyfication."

Jean-Louis Deotte analyzed contemporary culture as an on-going proliferation of the museum model to delimit any cultural activity: the separation and sublimation of objects or spaces which gain in distinction what they lose in reality. Disneyfication, conversely, partakes of this substitutory mechanism, though on the basis of the mediatic confusion between reality and simulation – thanks to which society and individuals avidly embrace the substitution of what is real by fiction – just as the substitution of the productive action is stimulated by the waste and extravagance of the game.

Micro compact car showrooms and sales centers for 100 European cities (1995)

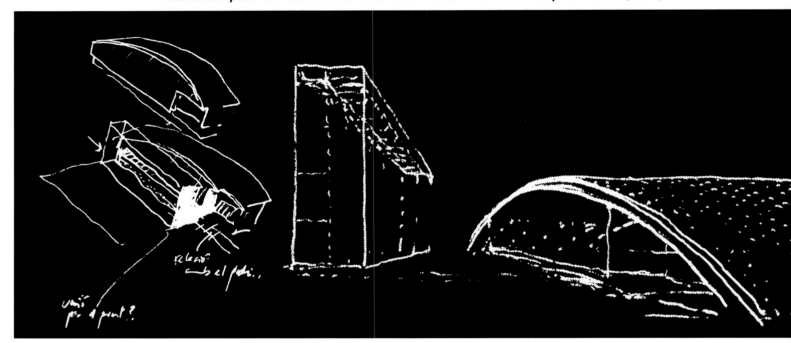

→This is the winning project in an invitational competition to design the prototype of a showroom and repair shop for the Micro Compact Car or SMART, the small car initially produced by a joint venture between Mercedes and Swatch. The basic conceptual approach was to define a big, shell-like unitary structure to house the repair shop and all its technical facilities and to display the stored cars on sale with their wide range of colors in a great glass front, which would become the main identifying image of the building and of the carmaker. The cars would thus be treated as delicate or precious small objects, protected in a glass box and gently handled by a robot which would bring the car to its prospective owner.
The brief called for a modular plan and ecological solutions to temperature control based on passive solar gain which would be able to respond to diverse climatic conditions in as many as 100 locations throughout Europe. A buffer zone and system of heat storage is provided by a double-cavity, curved roof which can be perforated to varying extents according to local climate conditions.
The evolution of the competition design in subsequent project phases tended towards the definition of more compact and economic layouts.

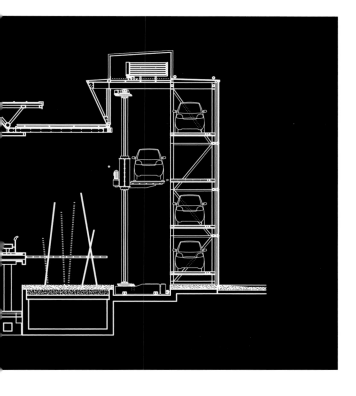

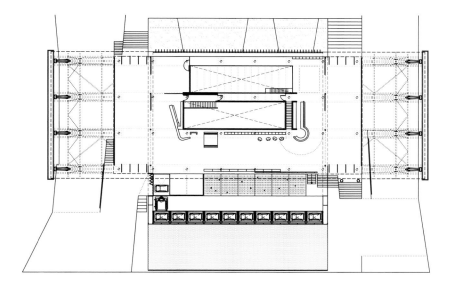

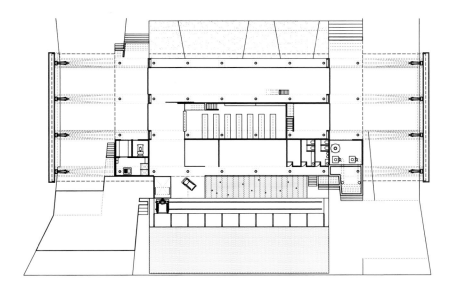

Competition stage. Floor plans and cross section through shell structure.
↑ Cross section of the display front. An existing standard system of storage is used.

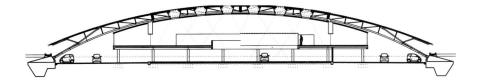

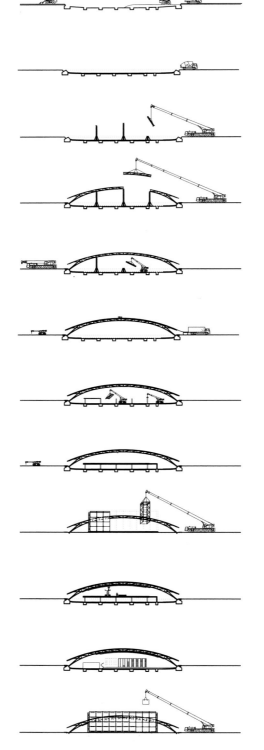

Views of the competition model and elevations.
↙ Schematic representation of the process of assembly. The shell roof is the first part to go up. This allows for the rest of the construction work to be carried out inside, sheltered from bad weather conditions. The display front is the last part to be assembled.

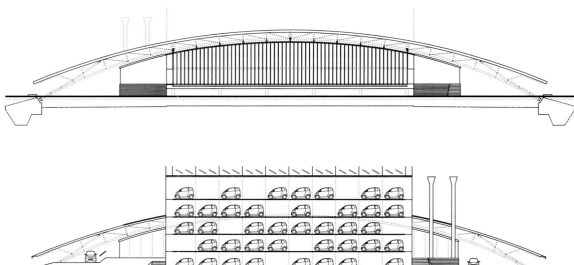

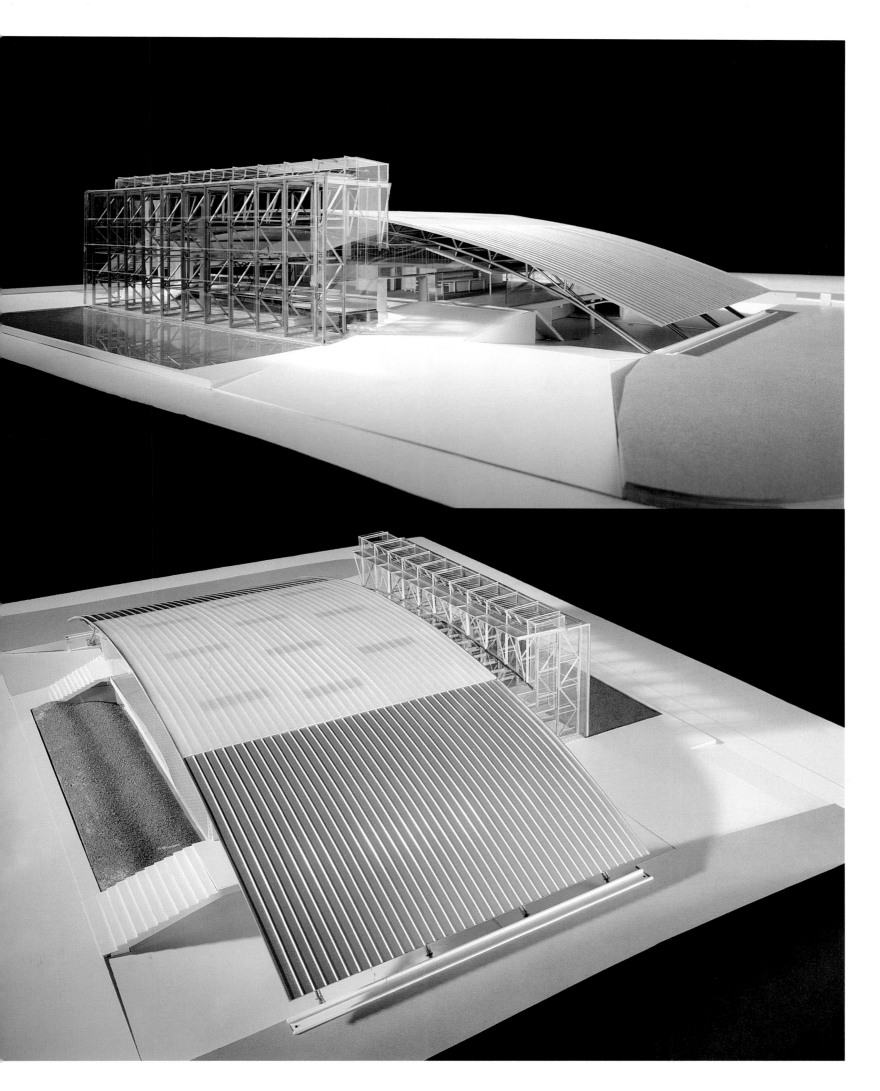

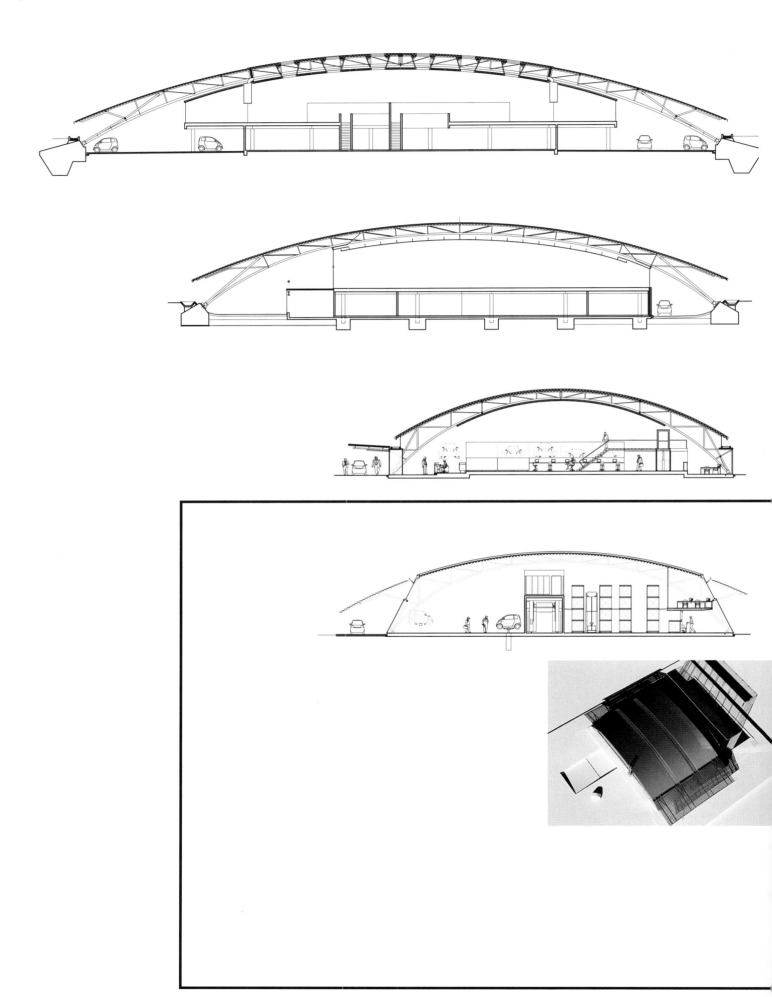

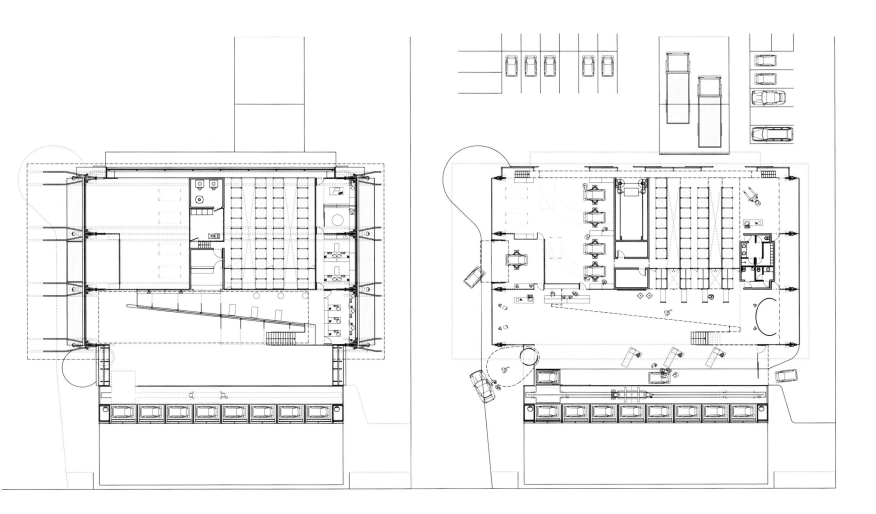

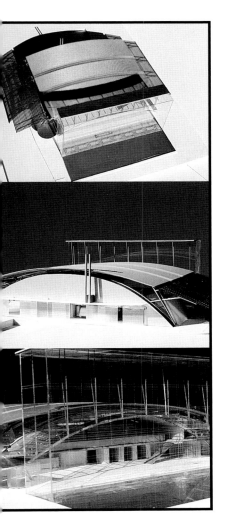

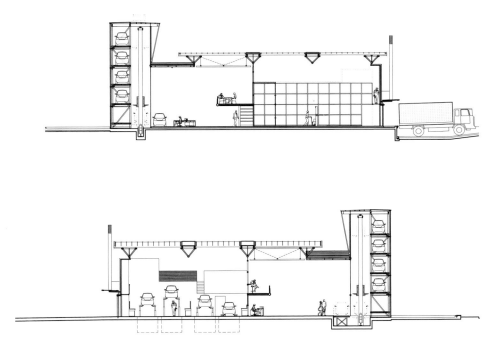

←Cross sections showing the evolution from the competition to the final design stages which reflects an effort to reduce the size and budget.
↑Floor plans and cross sections of the final design stage.

adidas stadium

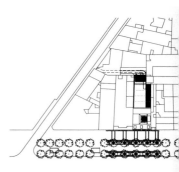

Shopping complex. Paris (1995)

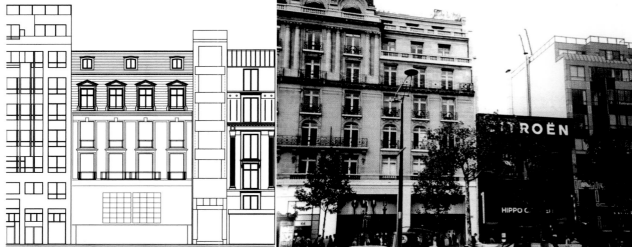

→Following the great success of other commercial sports brands, Adidas invited Jean Nouvel, Ron Arad and Alfredo Arribas to produce schemes for a large retail space that would simultaneously incorporate other leisure activities, such as a small theater for interactive projections and a café. The chosen site is an old building on the Champs Élysées which responds to the most strict Parisian tradition of mansard roofs and party walls. For this scheme Pierre Chareau's work at the Maison de Verre has been used as a reference, so that the two upper floors and the mansard roof are retained and the lower part of the building is hollowed out while most of the façade is preserved within a new glass case. The long cross section running perpendicular to the street front defines the spatial organization of the brief, with the theater hanging detached from the walls and ceilings in the center of a "promenade architecturale" established by a sequence of steps, escalators, catwalks and balconies flooded with daylight.

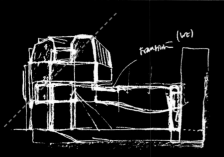

Frankfurt (VE)

←Sketch of the cross section.
↓Sketch, model, and detail cross
section of the glass case concept for
the façade.

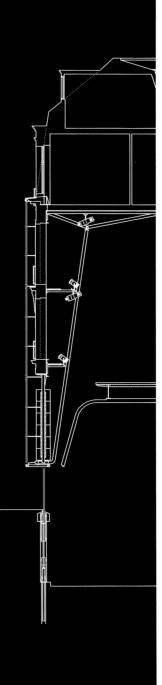

↖Site plan and view of the building on
the Champs Elysées.
←Views from the back courtyard of the
Maison de Verre before its renovation
and of the hollowed-out interior.

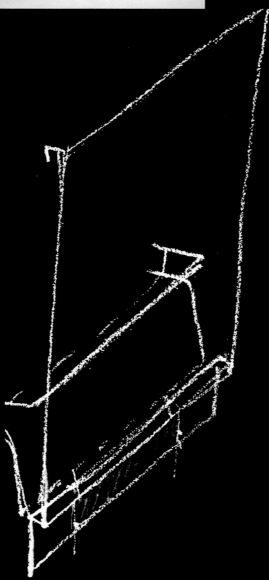

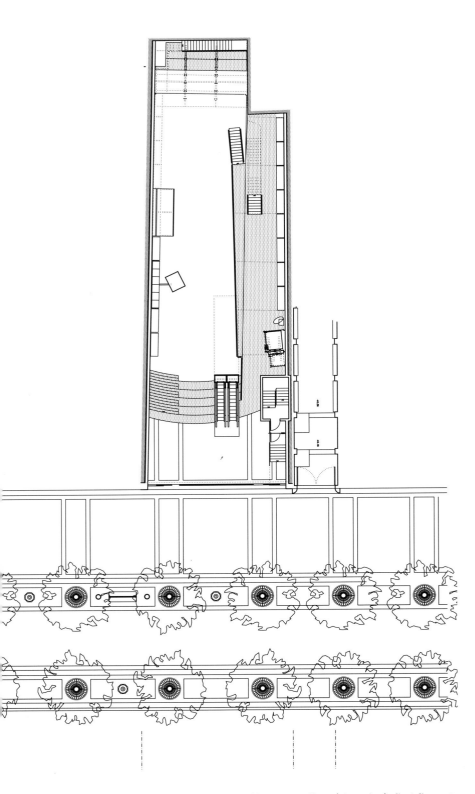

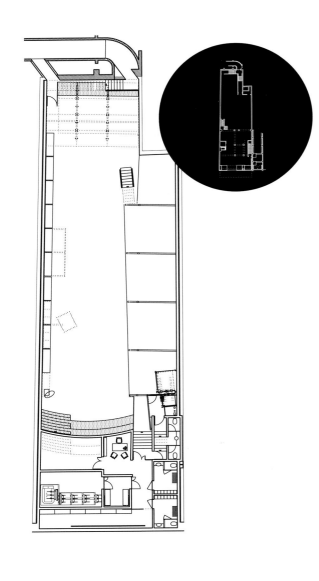

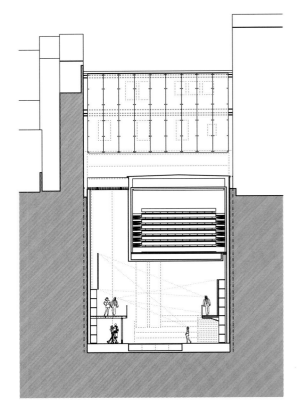

↑From left to right: entrance and basement floor (shopping), first floor at ground level (shopping and stair/ramp to the theater), second floor (sports café and entrance to the theater), third floor (theater, exit, and bar). The fourth and fifth floors contain offices. Circled in black: plans of the existing floors.

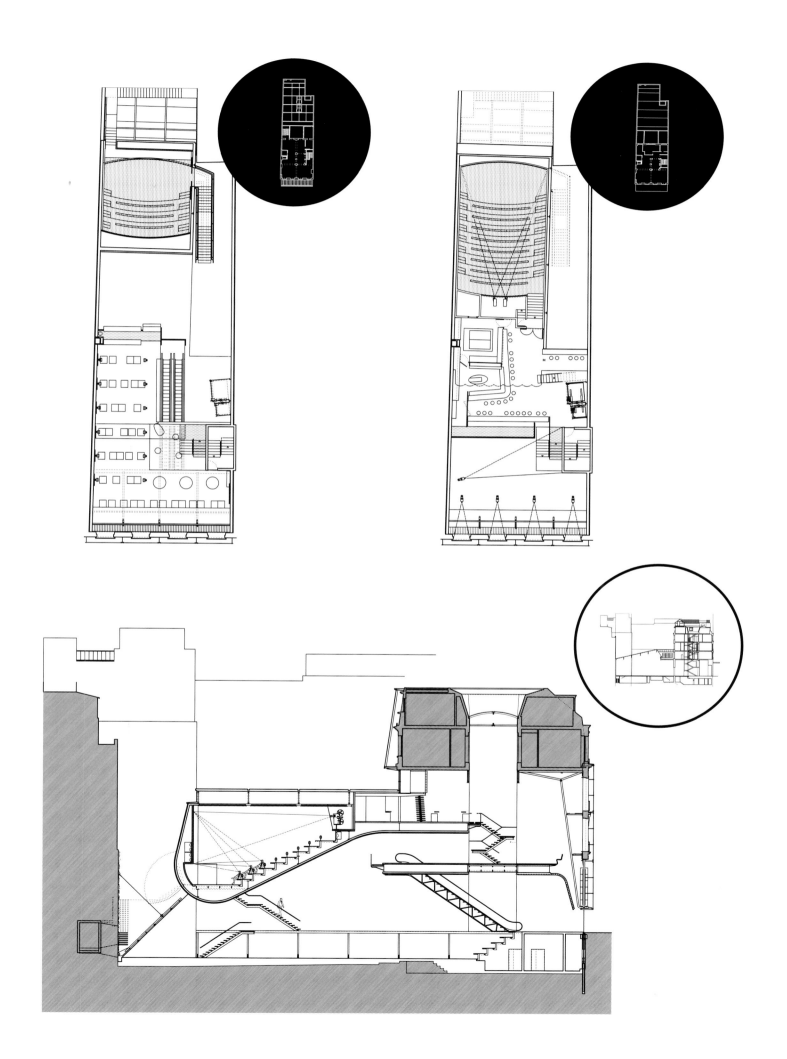

Views of the model and sketch of the central theater.

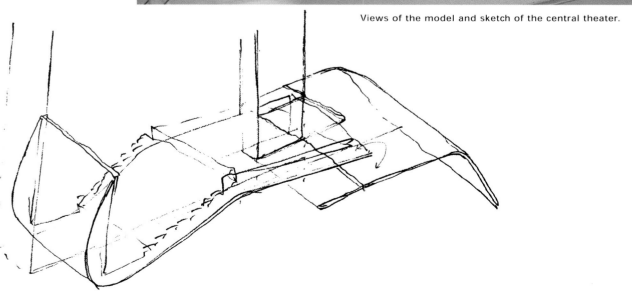

schwarzenbergplatz

Public space renovation. Vienna (1998-2001)

→ This project, which was the winning scheme of an urban design competition, has been intended as an enhancement of the existing signs and qualities of Schwarzenbergplatz, on the southern side of Vienna's 19th-century Ring. Paving materials in different shades of gray – asphalts, stone, concrete – define the ground plane in the daytime as a continuation of the neoclassical façades of this urban "salon," while the lighting design embedded in the ground reveals at nighttime the flow of the city and its inhabitants. The only overhead lighting is provided by new rows of indirect, diffuse street lamps on the central promenade that replace the existing lampposts on the sidewalks.

The rest of the lighting design creates a new dynamic ground configuration that interacts with passing streetcars and other vehicles. Streetcar stops and kiosks are grouped together at different points, and existing urban landmarks – the obelisk, the fountain and the statue – are emphatically illuminated by lights marking their bases. All the materials of the new architectural elements – glass, steel, and aluminum – multiply the effects of the light, be it daylight, headlights, street lights or advertising signs.

↑ Views of the site (Schwarzenbergplatz and of the "Hippodrom" with the obelisk in the background) and project perspective.
↓ The site plan below shows the southern part of the Ring.

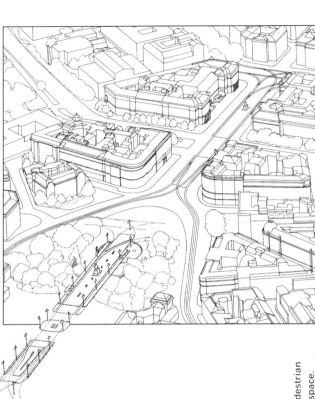

↓ Night perspective. Flashing red lights between the rails warn of the proximity of a streetcar, pedestrian crosswalks are marked by fluorescent green lights, and a central beam of light unifies the whole space.

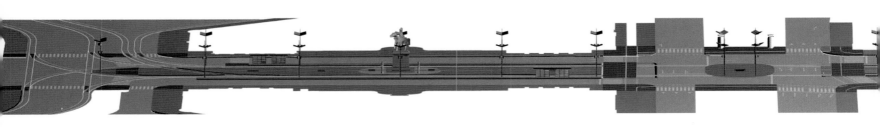

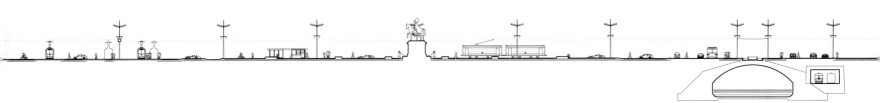

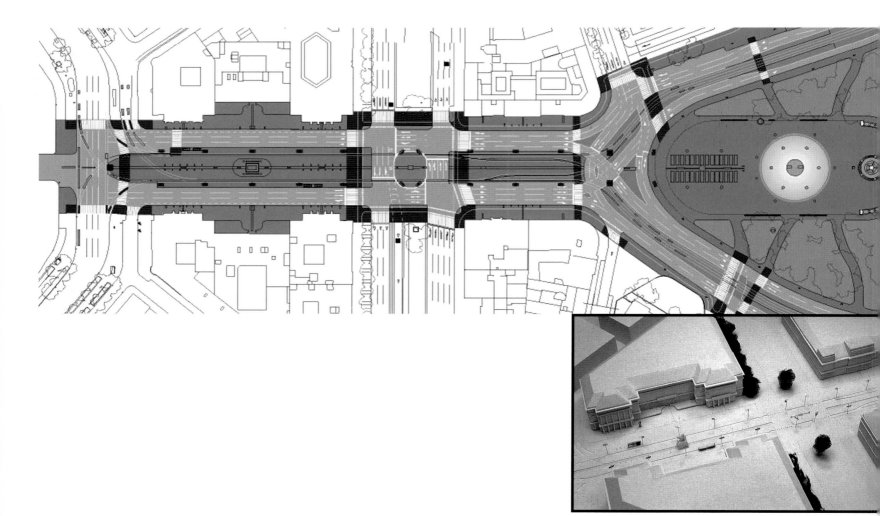

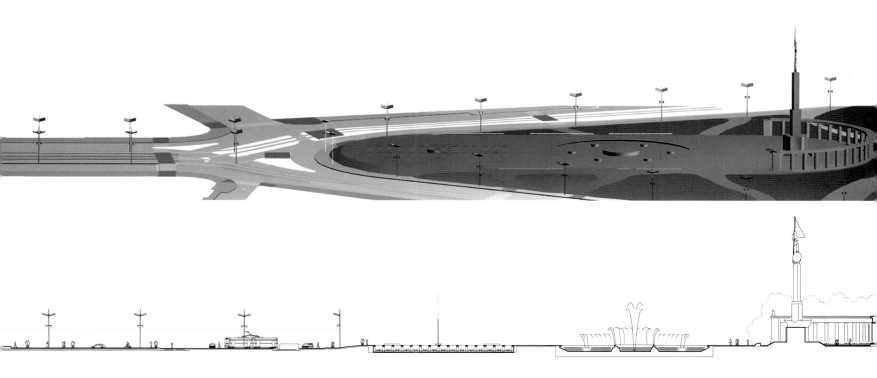

Perspective and longitudinal section. The plans show the changing spatial
perceptions as the light "machines" embedded in the surfaces are revealed.
Left, the urban order during the daytime. Right, the dynamic flow at nighttime.

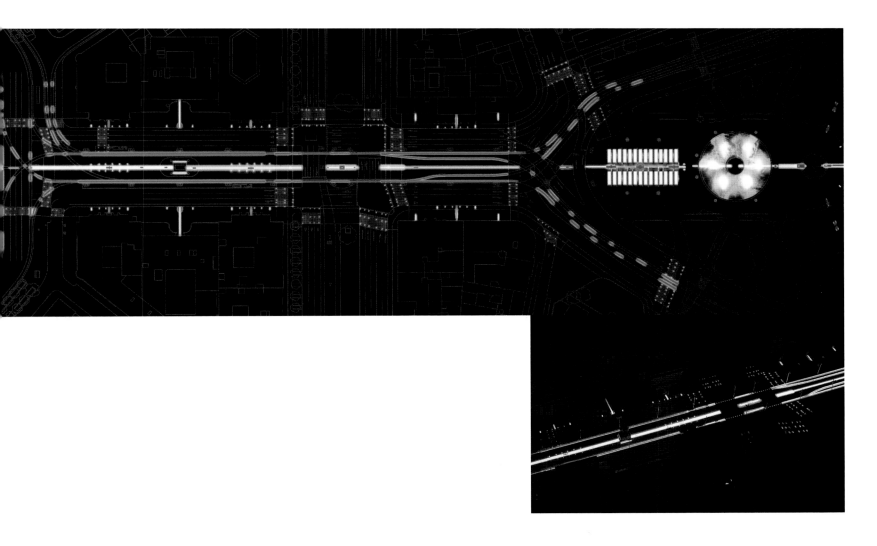

Museum, auditorium, and research center. Montluçon (1998-2003)

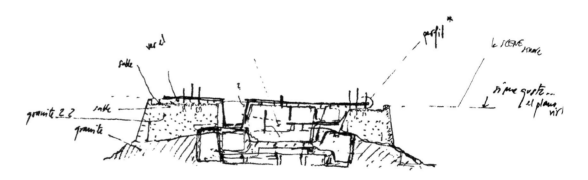

→The museum of "living music" has been simultaneously conceived as a leisure and educational center and a reference point for contemporary musical culture in Europe. This project was the winning scheme in a competition which was also seen as a fundamental tool in the renovation of the castle and the center of Montluçon. The project responds to the presence of the fortress and its central void – a historically secluded space at the top of a hill, with spectacular views of the city and the whole region – by locating all of the new construction underground in the large esplanade which faces Château des Ducs de Bourbon, the museum's symbolic gate. The existing street system and stairs have been improved, extended, and carved into the hill to enhance public use and the integration of this space in the urban fabric. Following the image of a music box, the hillock's granite mass is hollowed out to create a large continuous space shaped by the flowing movement of sound, natural light, and the museum visitors. This container is covered by a granite platform – a symbolic surface which calls for public participation and which is slightly tilted to create a continuous gap on one of the sides, thus revealing its contents and allowing daylight to be filtered in. Inside, the underground museum spaces are organized into a sequence of independent, enclosed, and acoustically insulated volumes which are freely arranged under the large roof and whose relative positions modulate the visitors' itinerary. One of these volumes, which houses a musical auditorium, is revealed to the city through a perforation on the rocky hillside.

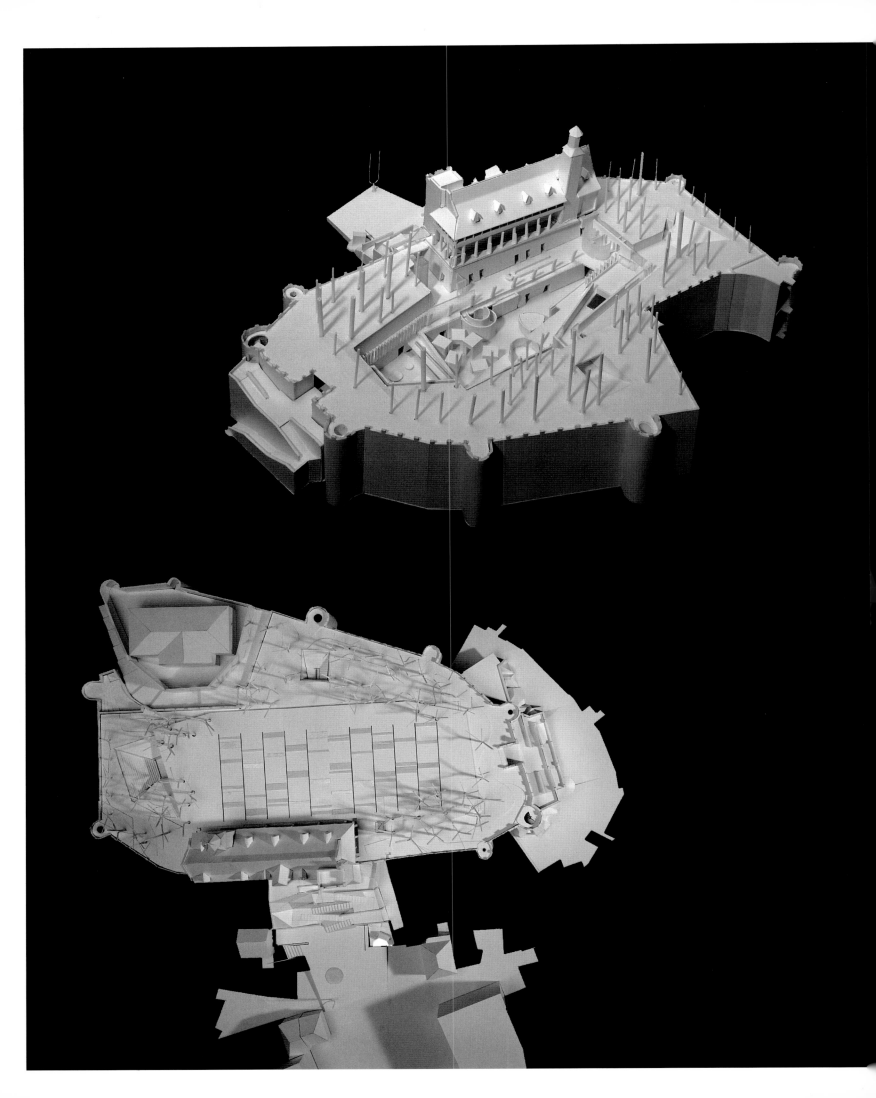

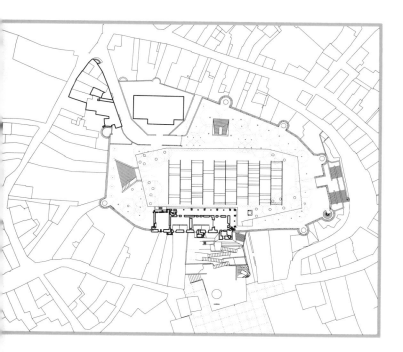

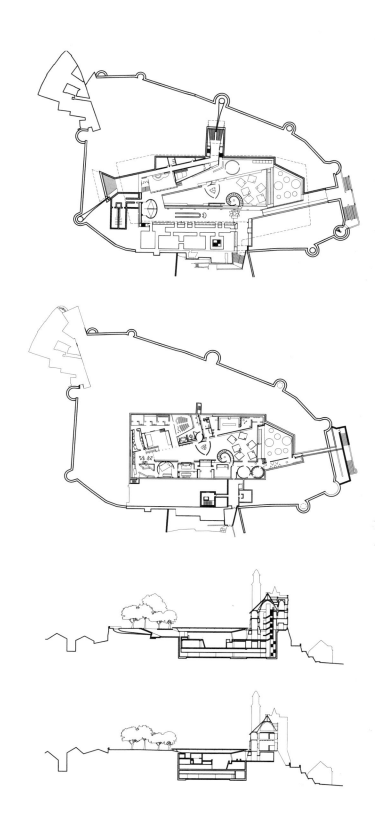

Competition stage. The museum program is organized into a sequence of independent volumes under a unitary roof which defines the esplanade as a "scène instrumentale," a public space in the form of a musical score activated by users' participation.

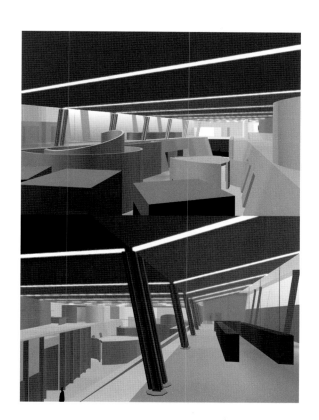

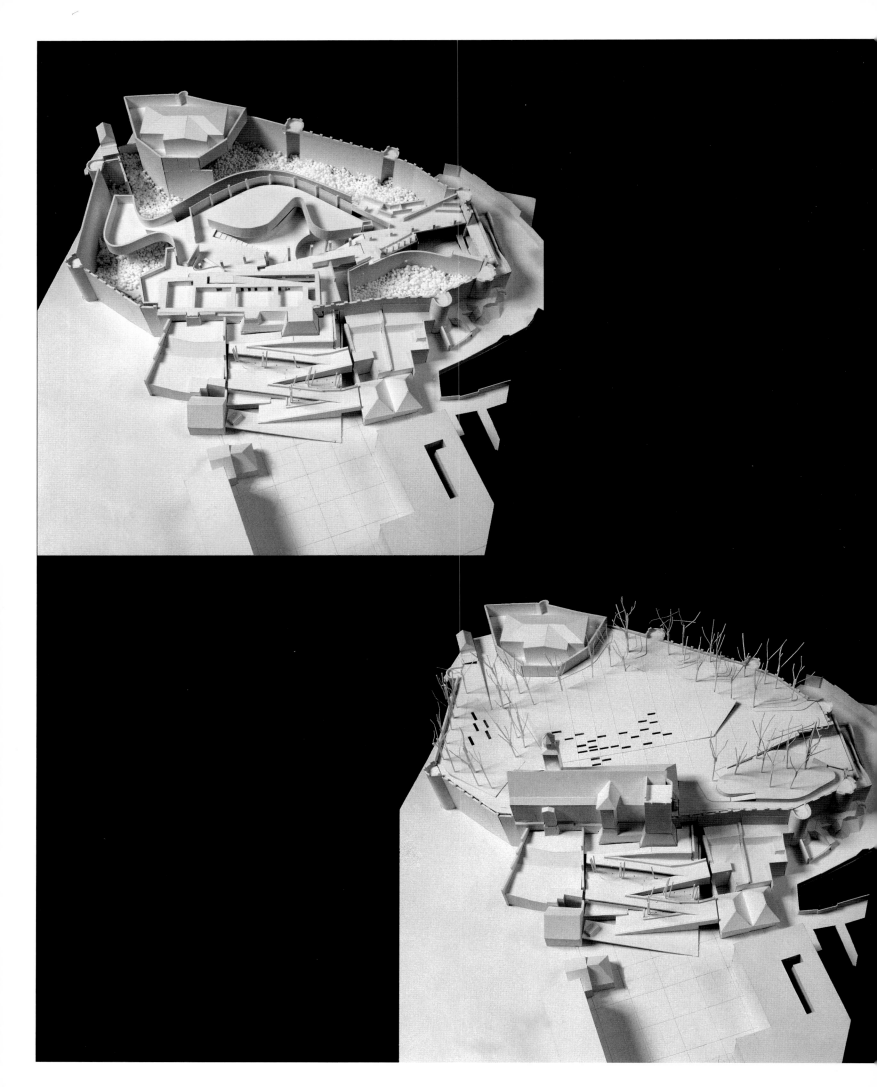

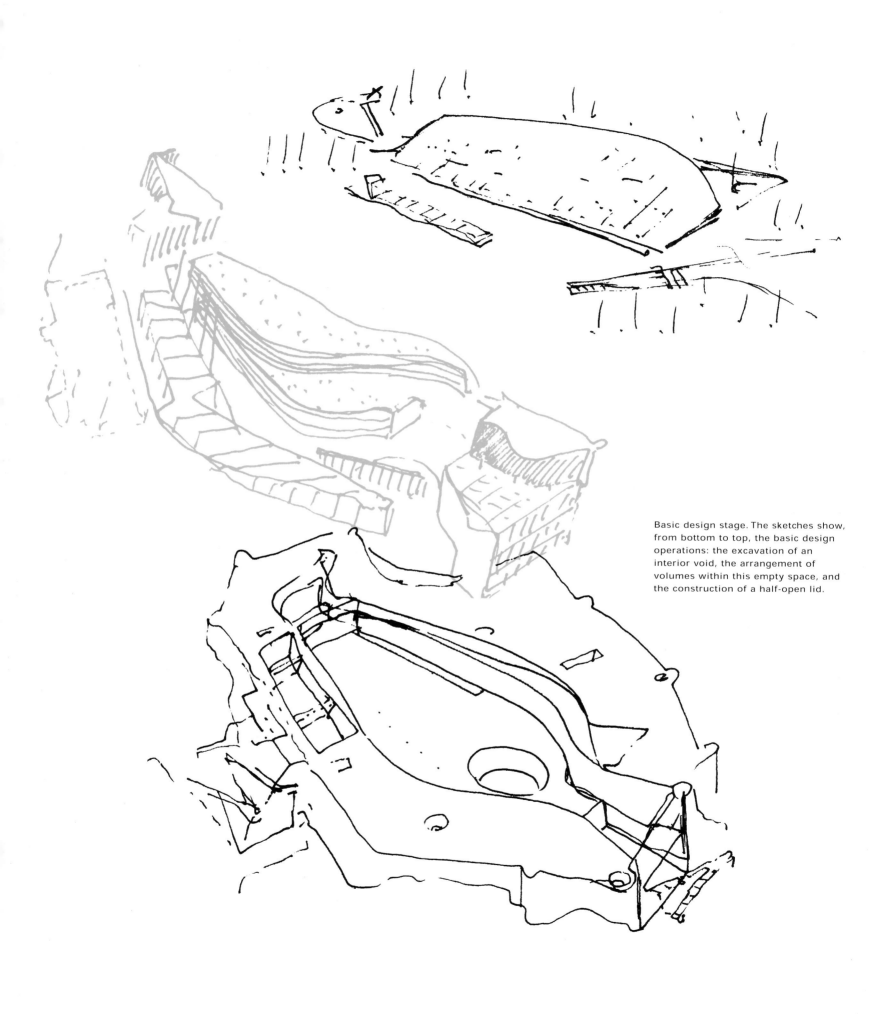

Basic design stage. The sketches show, from bottom to top, the basic design operations: the excavation of an interior void, the arrangement of volumes within this empty space, and the construction of a half-open lid.

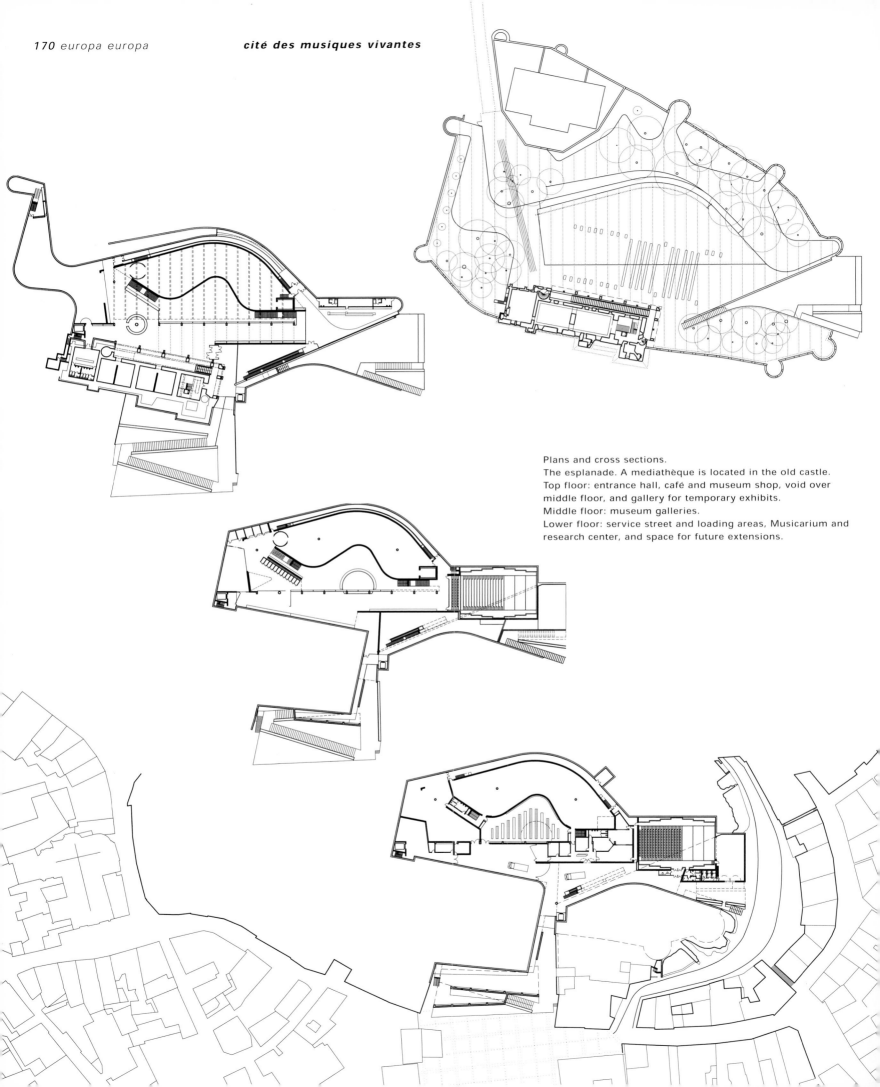

Plans and cross sections.
The esplanade. A mediathèque is located in the old castle.
Top floor: entrance hall, café and museum shop, void over middle floor, and gallery for temporary exhibits.
Middle floor: museum galleries.
Lower floor: service street and loading areas, Musicarium and research center, and space for future extensions.

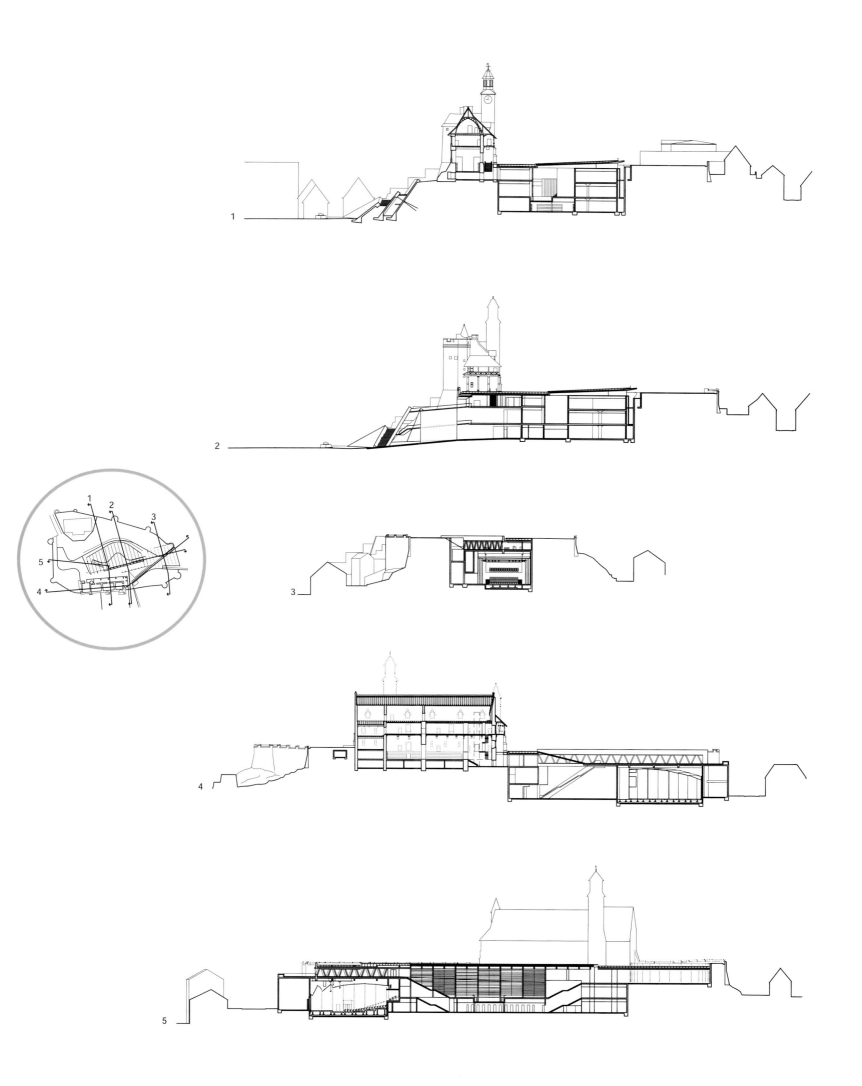

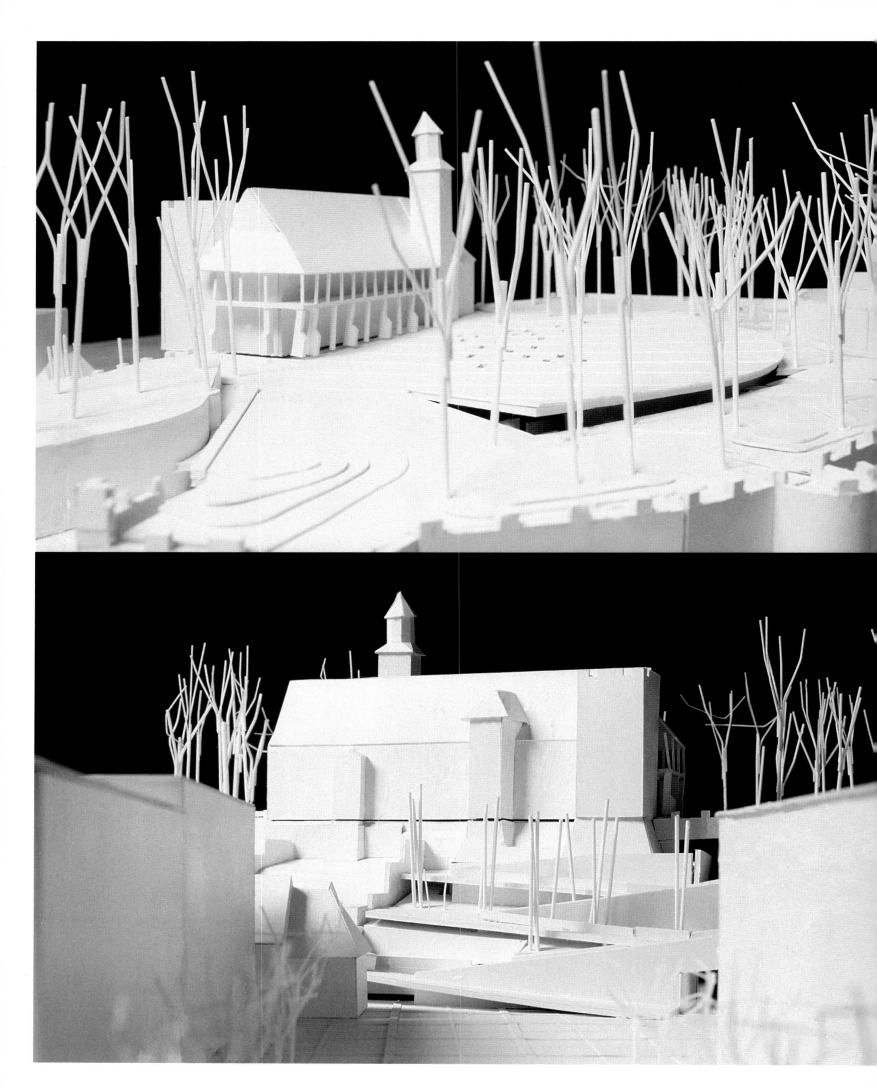

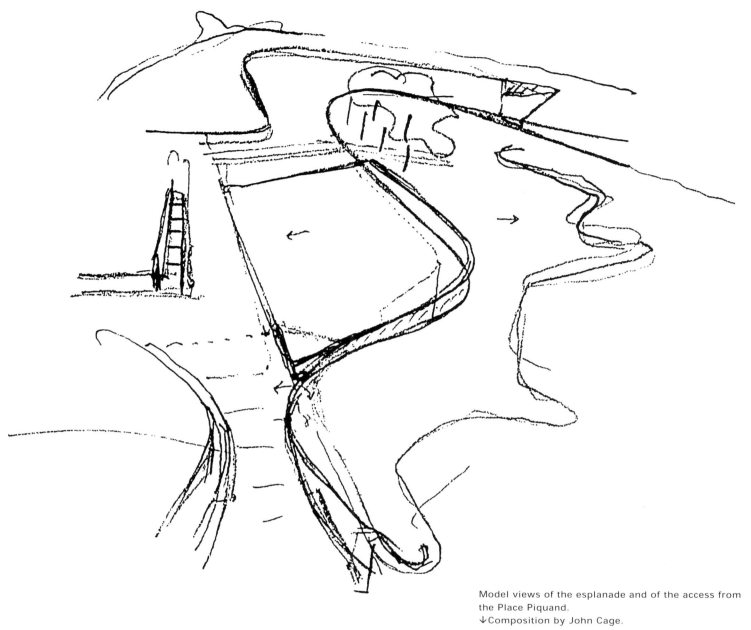

Model views of the esplanade and of the access from
the Place Piquand.
↓Composition by John Cage.

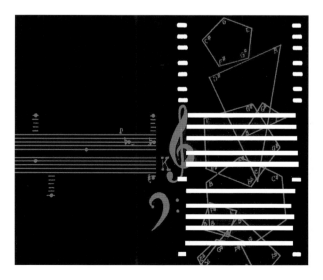

feli.città

*With Javier Mariscal
and Dani Freixes*

Family entertainment center and Imax theater. Castellaneta-Bari (1997-2001)

→This family theme park is part of a large tourist development on the southern Italian coast, at the fringe of a protected wooded landscape. The master plan drawn by Emilio Ambasz also included a preliminary design for the park, which sought to integrate an Imax theater and other family amenities into the protected surroundings by creating a natural landscape in which most spaces would be located underground. The thematic elaboration developed in collaboration with artist Javier Mariscal and architect Dani Freixes defines what can be seen as the recently discovered conglomeration of the half-buried buildings of a timeless city. A circular ridge delimits the public edge and access areas to the park and incorporates a ring of services and a panoramic walkway around this imaginary city and its central lake. Two contrasting volumes rise above the surface at either end of the park – a truncated cone and a square block which house the Imax theater and an arena respectively. These two poles of the sequence of amenities are linked by a podium which contains large underground spaces for games and thematic exhibitions and protrudes on the lakeside from within the broken volumetric configuration of the urban scenery. In contrast to the massive look of these buildings, the structure and appearance of the Imax theater and the arena are defined by the use of steel frames and a system of cables and hanging trusses which reinterpret the volumetric definition of Ambasz's original project.

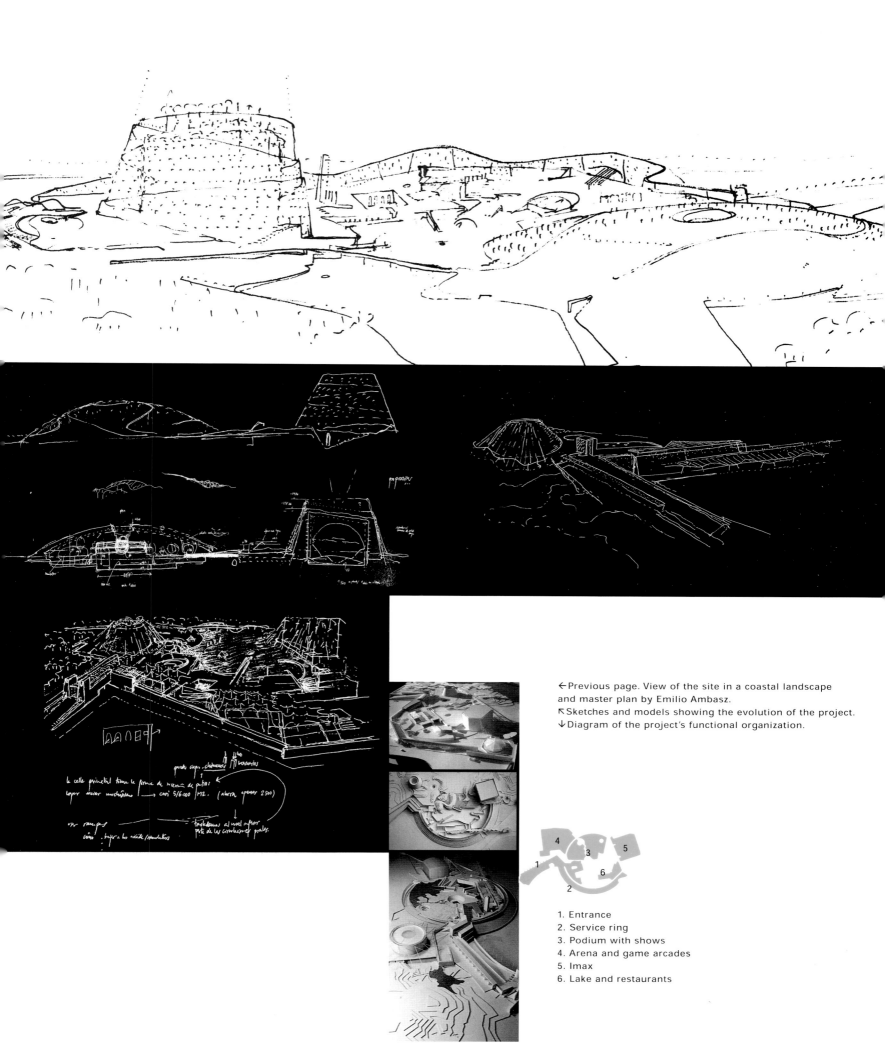

←Previous page. View of the site in a coastal landscape
and master plan by Emilio Ambasz.
↖Sketches and models showing the evolution of the project.
↓Diagram of the project's functional organization.

1. Entrance
2. Service ring
3. Podium with shows
4. Arena and game arcades
5. Imax
6. Lake and restaurants

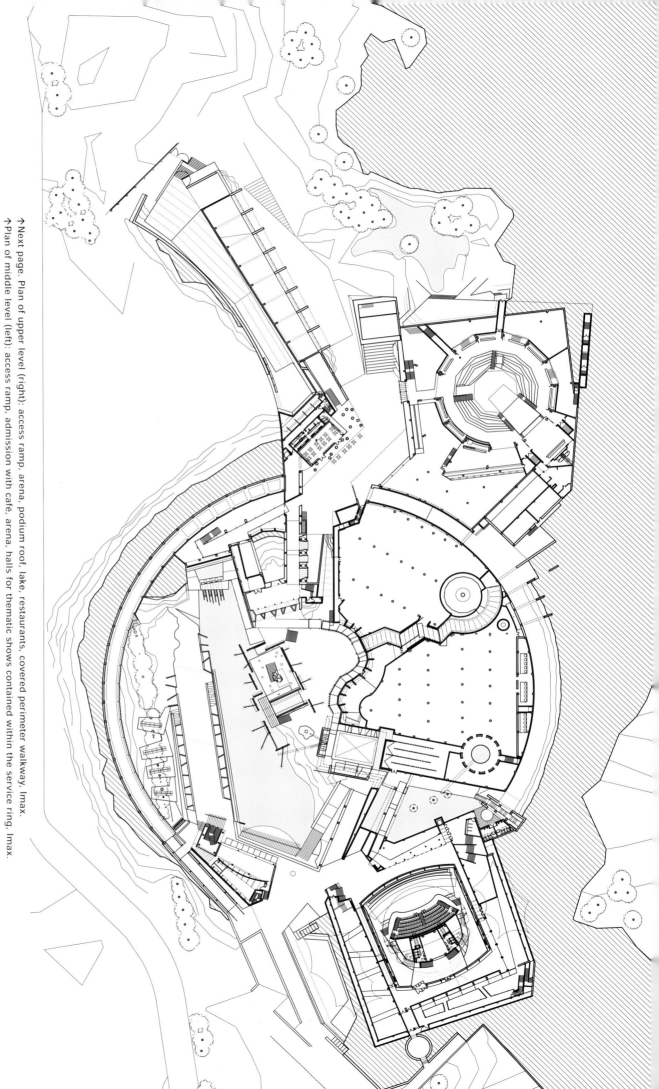

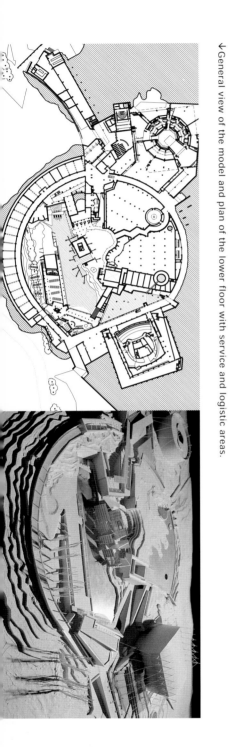

↑Next page. Plan of upper level (right): access ramp, arena, podium roof, lake, restaurants, covered perimeter walkway, Imax.
↑Plan of middle level (left): access ramp, admission with café, arena, halls for thematic shows contained within the service ring, Imax.
↓General view of the model and plan of the lower floor with service and logistic areas.

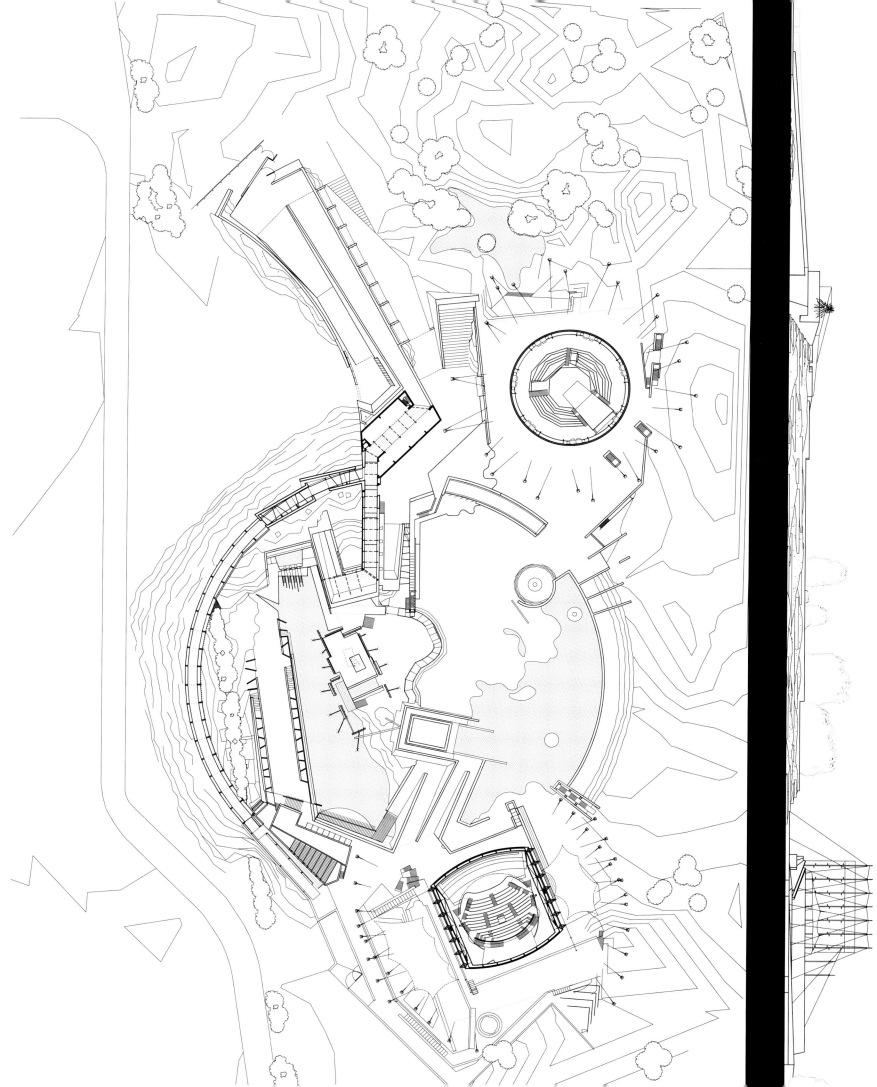

View of the fragmented volumes surrounding the lake and the circling embankment defined by the service street and the perimeter walkway.

View of the model with the Imax theater on the left and the disco/arena on the right.
The section shows the connecting podium between them, which will fill the excavated
area shown in the construction photograph.

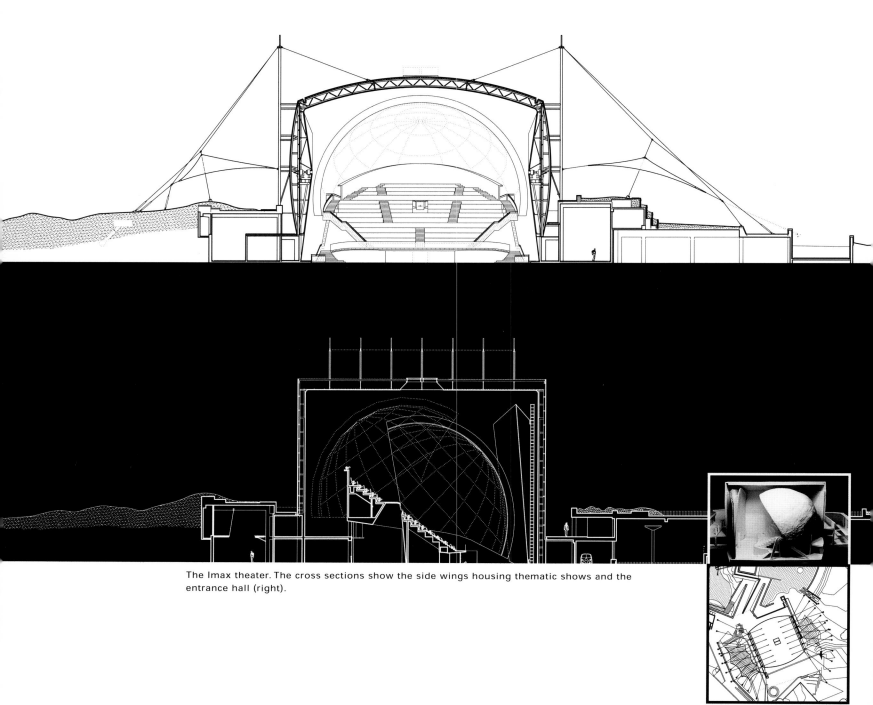

The Imax theater. The cross sections show the side wings housing thematic shows and the entrance hall (right).

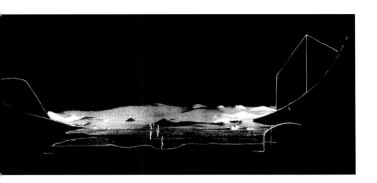

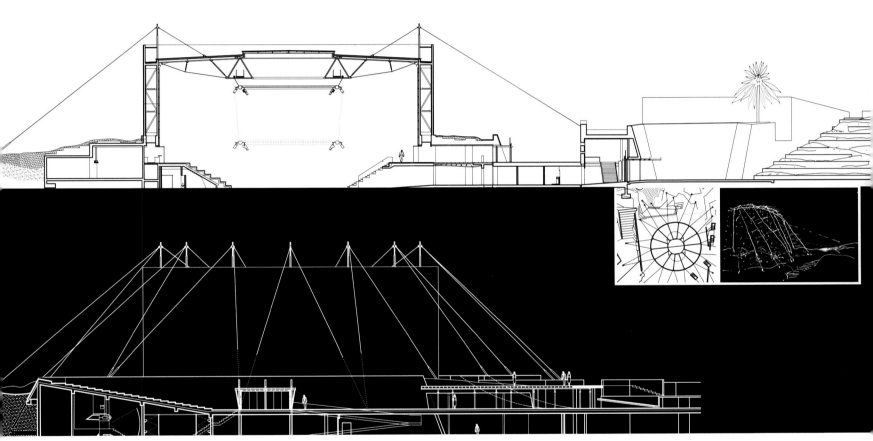

The arena. The cross sections show the access system from the outside (right) and the ring of bars (left).

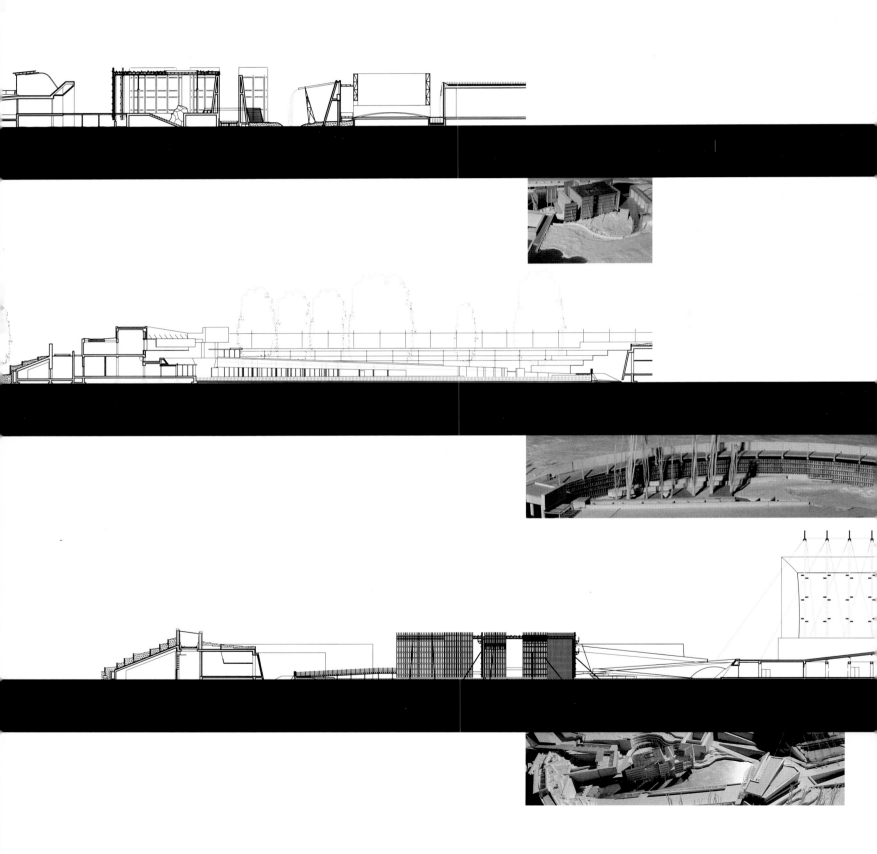

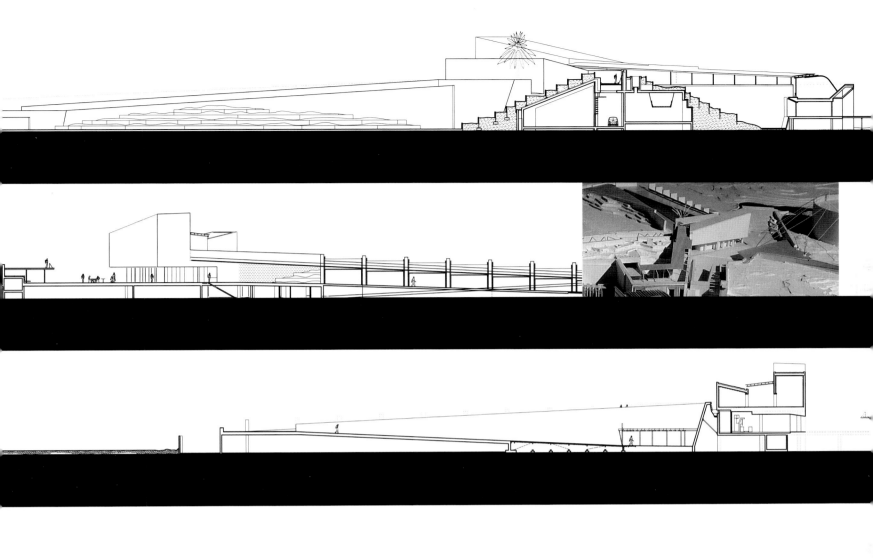

Cross sections showing the fragmentary condition of the project.

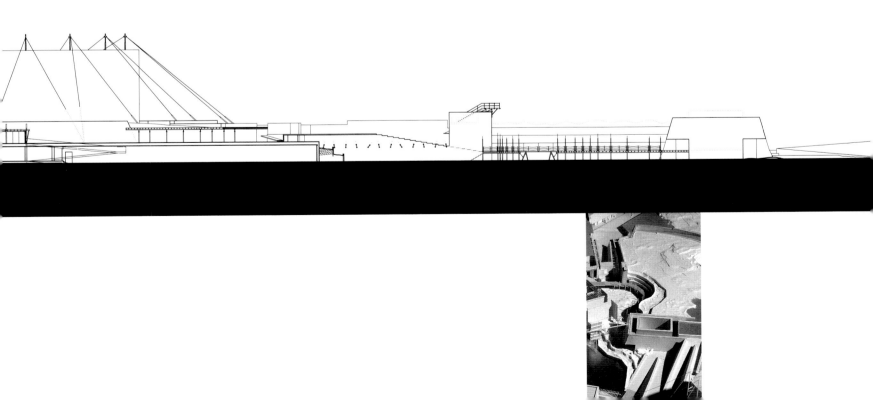

seat-stadt pavilion

Multimedia pavilion in Volkswagen's Autostadt. Wolfsburg (1998-2000)

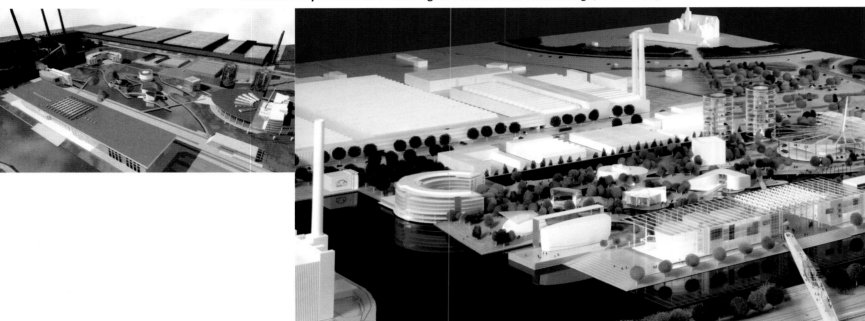

Autostadt is a theme park built by Volkswagen in part of its original Wolfsburg plant. The park (together with a forum, a museum, a hotel and a delivery center) includes independent pavilions for Volkwagen's sister companies in Europe. These pavilions are integrated within a landscaped promenade that defines the visitor's path, and each has been designed by architects from the respective company's country. From the project's early sketches, the Seat pavilion has tried to be an expression of movement instead of a static building, thus, its curved shapes generate a multiplicity of appearances depending on the point from which the building is seen. The visitors are taken high above the ground by means of a curving ramp and are led, in an effort to emphasize the perception of the building's size, into the center of the pavilion's longitudinal axis. An interior architecture of cylinders and ramps organizes the visit in a downward movement through multimedia presentations. The building's white interior architecture is wrapped by a simple steel-frame construction, which allows for a flexible disposition of skylights, and is clad in an outer skin of small round ceramic tiles.

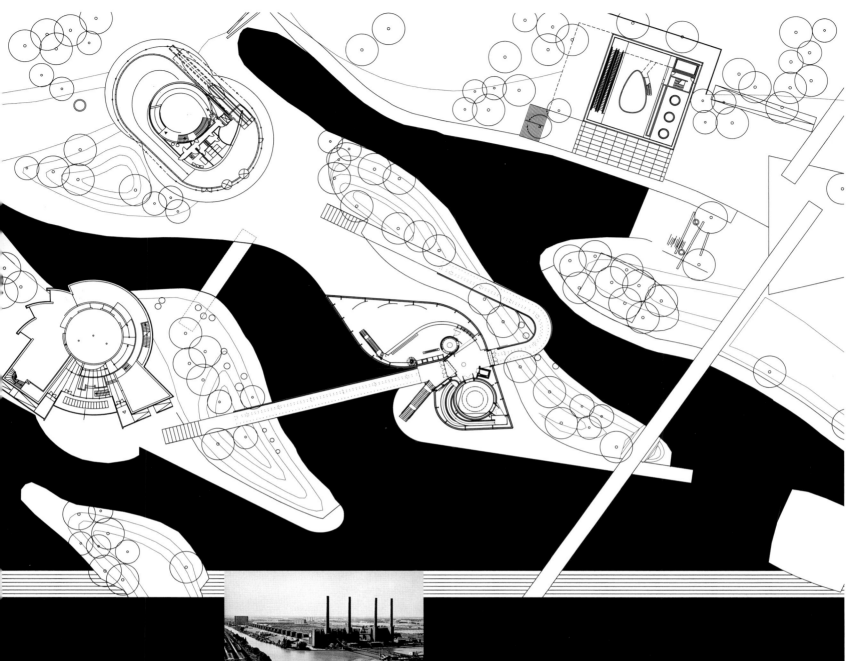

↖Computer rendering and model of Volkswagen's Autostadt next to its emblematic
Wolfsburg plant.
↑The Seat pavilion is shown in the site plan as a connective element
in the park's plan.

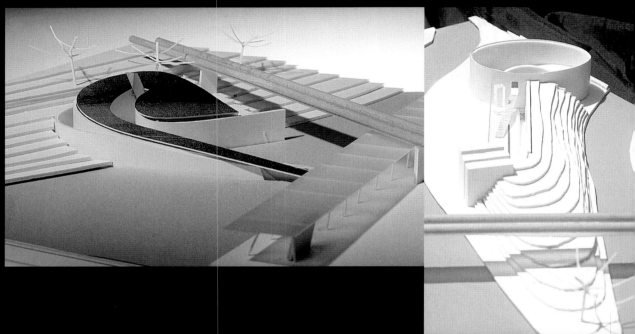

Models and sketches of preliminary design concepts.

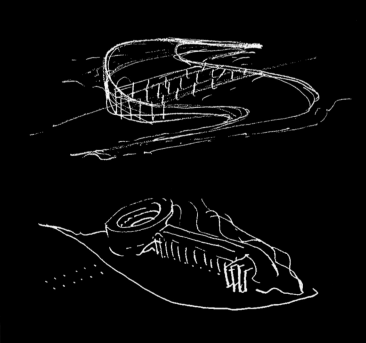

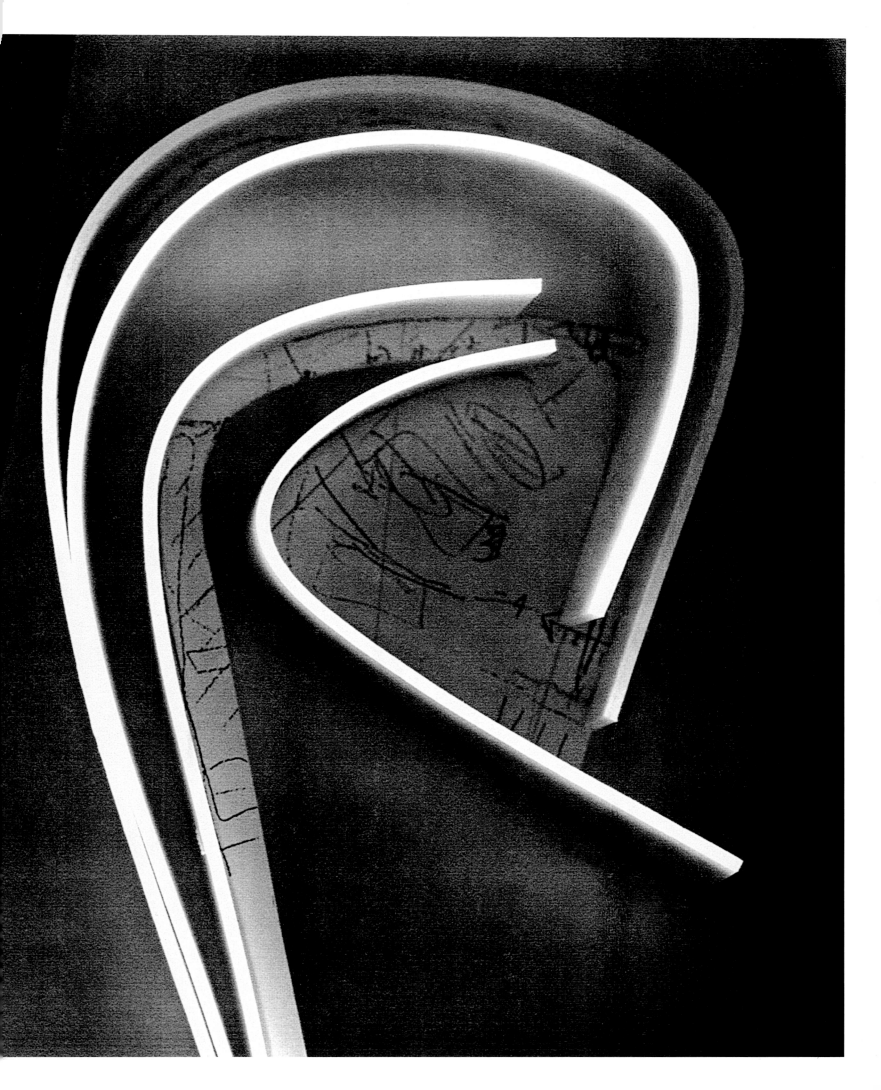

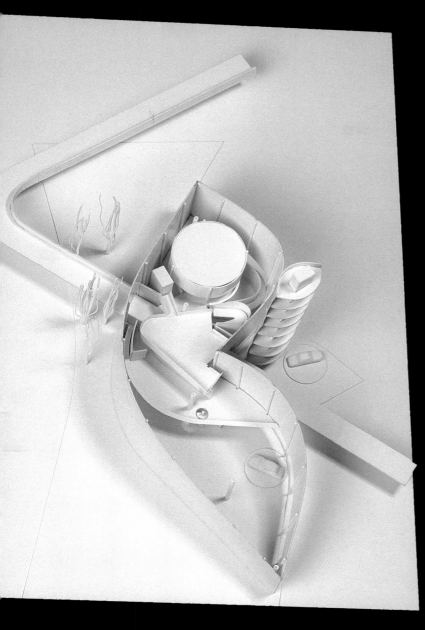

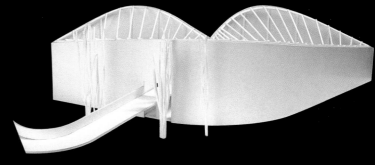

Study models of the final proposal.
←Model of the roof structure.

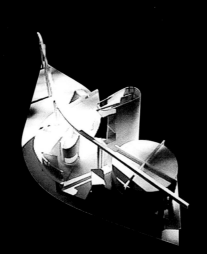

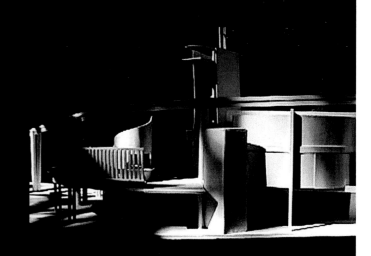

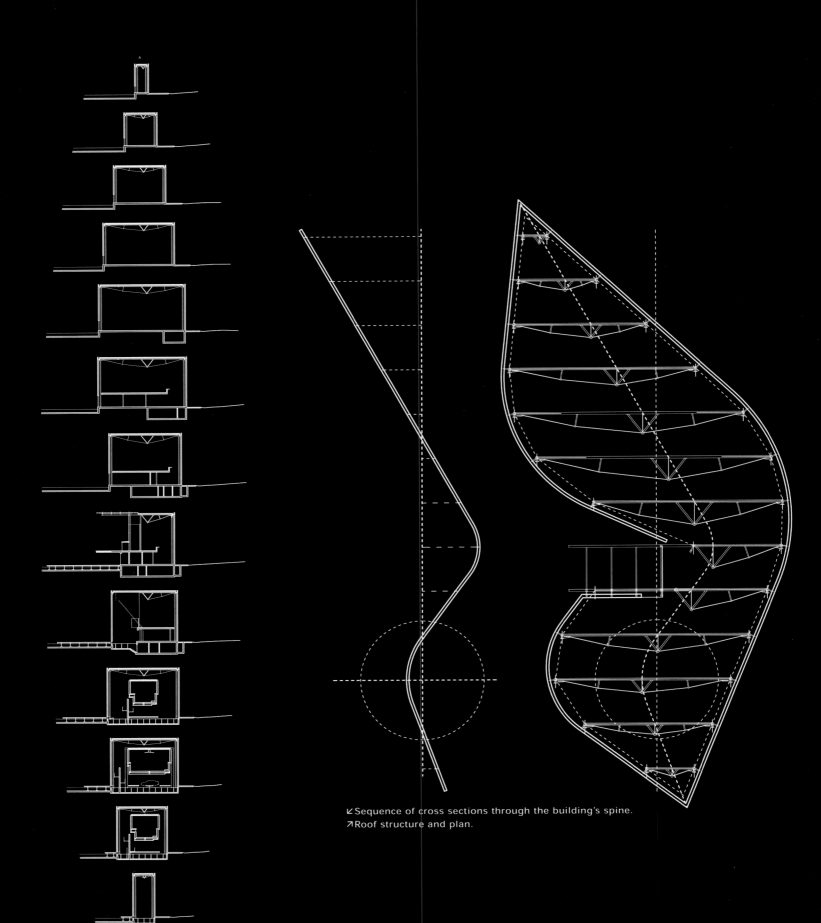

↙ Sequence of cross sections through the building's spine.
↗ Roof structure and plan.

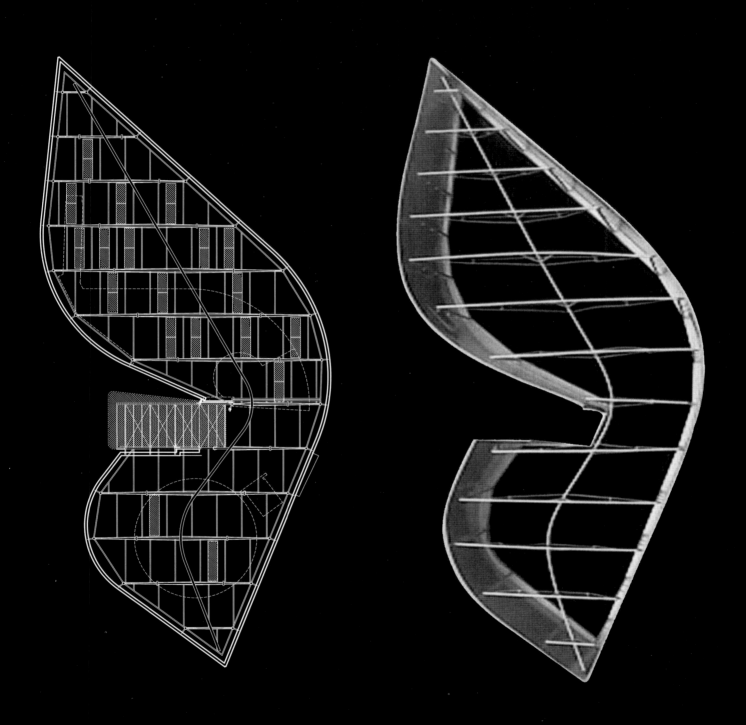

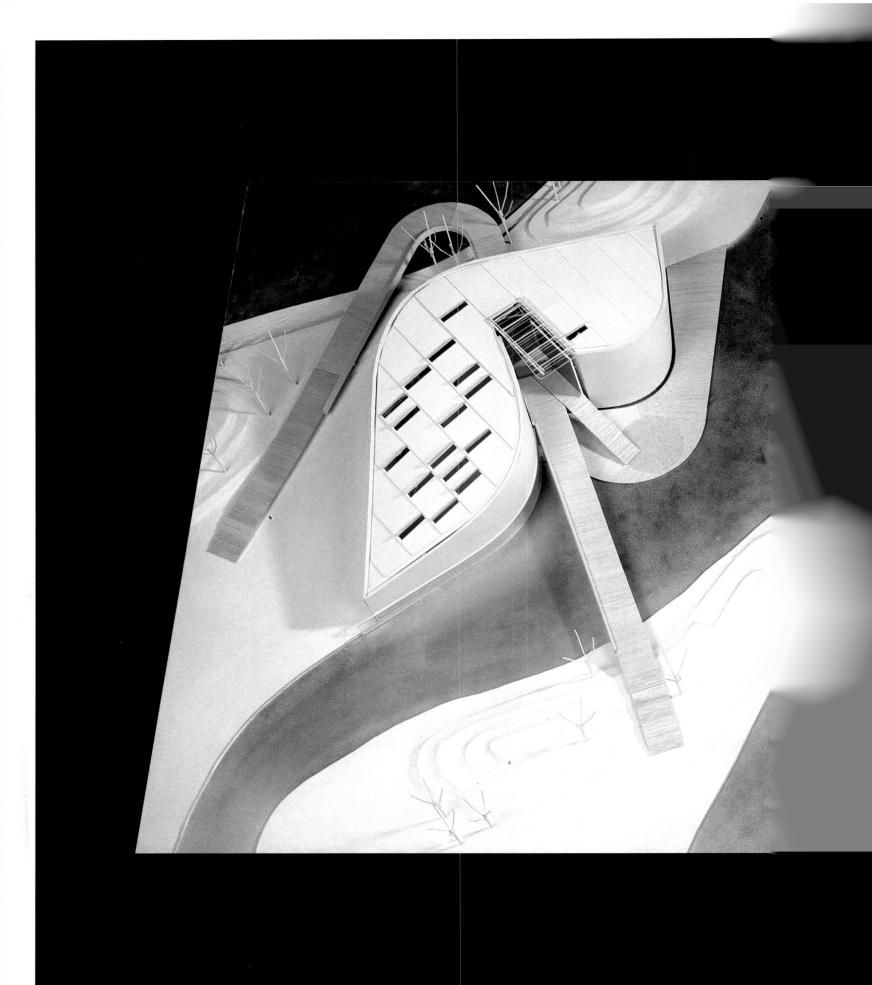

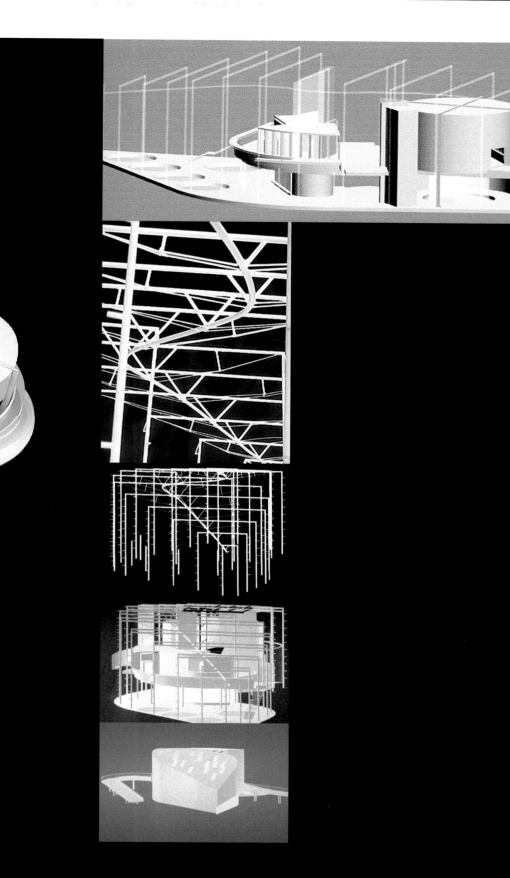

The study models and computer renderings show the definition of the pavilion's interior architecture, the structural frame that defines the container, and the outer skin.

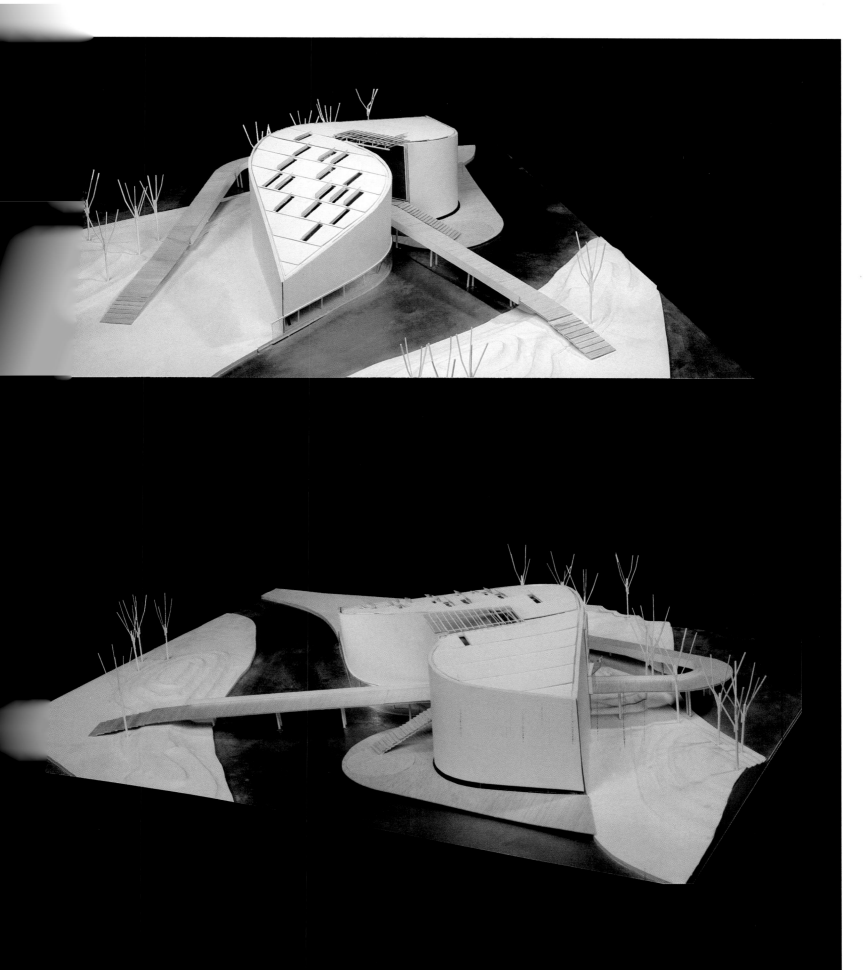

↑ Counterclockwise from top left: renderings of the entrance, ramp around the cyclorama, interactive games on the ground floor, and showroom with the information space above it. ↓ Exterior view of the built skin.

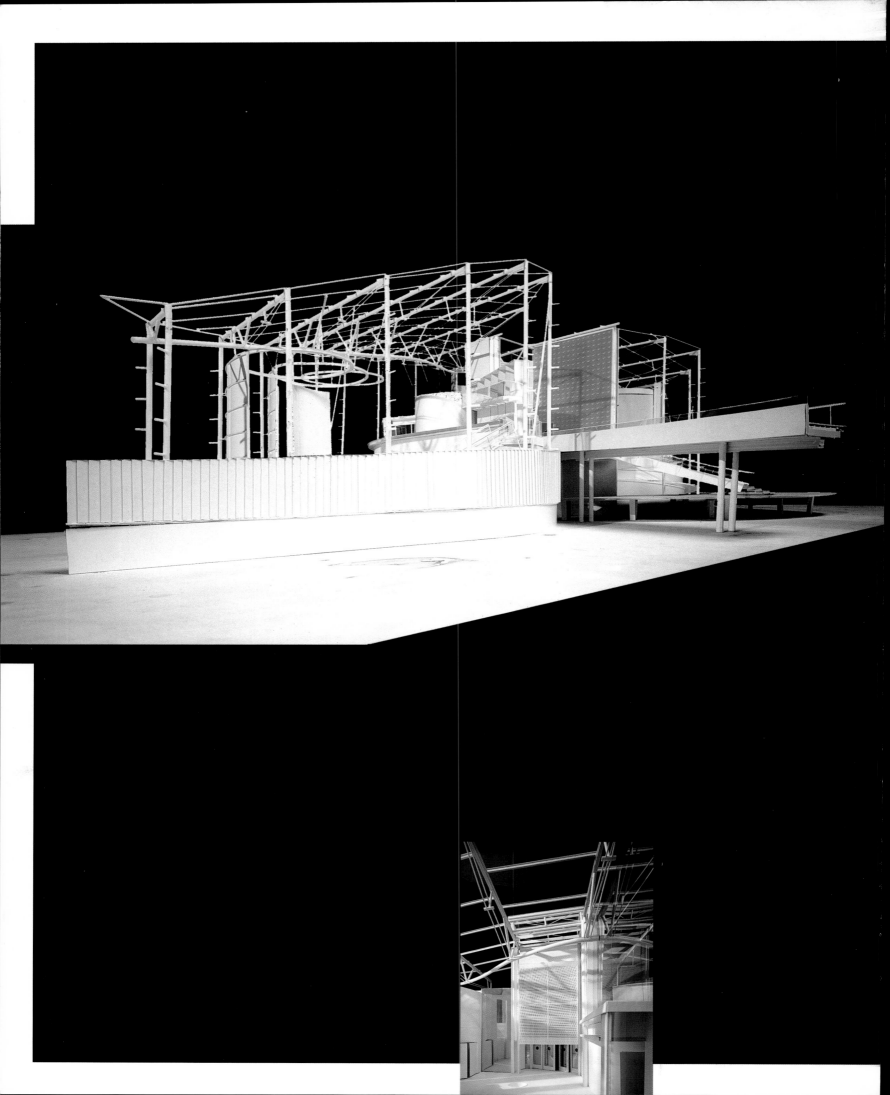

chronology of works

2000

Fundació Puigvert.
Urban Planning and New Building for
Medical Services, Hospital de Sant Pau.
Barcelona, Spain.
2000-02

Glass Pavilion.
Frankfurt Zoo.
Frankfurt, Germany.
2000-01

Maremàgnum.
Urban Planning and Extension of a
Leisure Center.
Old Harbor, Barcelona, Spain.
First Prize in Limited Competition.
2000-04

1999

Corporate Office Building.
Terrassa, Barcelona, Spain.
Project 1999

Trend Hotel.
Exhibition Domotex Fair.
Hannover, Germany.
1999

Casa Buget.
Premià de Mar, Barcelona, Spain.
1999-2001

Big Fun.
Family Entertainment Centers.
Design Program 1999-2000

Salones.
Bar-Café-Arcade.
Design Program 1999-2000

1998

Seat-Stadt Pavilion.
Volkswagen AG. Autostadt.
Wolfsburg, Germany.
Construction 1998-2000

Seat Dealers New Centers.
Architecture & Showroom program.
1998-2000

Schwarzenbergplatz.
Public Space Renovation.
Vienna, Austria.
1998-2000

Sant Nicolau School.
Extension.
Sabadell, Barcelona, Spain.
Project 1998

1997

Lehrter Bahnhof.
Railway Station.
Berlin, Germany.
Project 1997

Feli.città.
Family Entertainment Center
and Imax Theater.
Bari, Italy.
Construction 2000-02

Contemporary Restaurant.
Peninsula Hotel. Jakarta, Indonesia.
First Prize in Limited Competition.
Project 1997

Cité des Musiques Vivantes.
Museum.
Montluçon, France.
First Prize in Limited Competition.
1998-2003

Urban Planning Piher Factory Area
and New Buildings.
Badalona, Barcelona, Spain.
Project 1997

1996

Commerzbank Plaza.
Entrance Hall, Main Lobby and Buffet
Restaurant in the Commerzbank
Zentrale Building.
Frankfurt, Germany.
Construction 1996-97

Fun Factory.
Entertainment and Sports Park.
Leipzig, Germany.
Project 1995-96

Art-Hotel.
Hotel Renovation and Extension.
Wiesbaden, Germany.
Project 1995-96

Meyer House & Paulus House.
Homes for two Families in Coto la
Zagaleta Benhavis.
Málaga, Spain.
Project 1996-98

Project for a Branch of Jewellery
Shops.
Barcelona, Spain.
Project 1996

Restaurant & Art Gallery.
KAI16 Building.
Düsseldorf, Germany.
Project 1996

Sky Trance International House of
Music Building.
Antwerp, Belgium.
Project 1996-98

Zeppelin Stuttgart Carré Restaurant.
Stuttgart, Germany.
First Prize in Limited Competition.
1996-97

Armazems do Chiado.
Lisbon, Portugal.
Limited Competition. 1996-97

1995

Bar. Maremàgnum.
Old Harbor, Barcelona, Spain.
Project 1995

Bockenheimer Depot.
Café and Theatre Hall. DAS TAT.
Frankfurt, Germany.
Project 1995

Euronet/Euromall.
Glass Pavilion, Garden, Food Court and
Shopping Center. Eurotower Building.
Frankfurt, Germany.
Construction 1995-96

Jazz Club.
Thessaloniki, Greece.
Project 1995

New Airport Lounges Lufthansa.
First Prize in Limited Competition 1995

MCC Smart.
Micro Compact Car Showrooms and
Sales Centers for 100 European Cities.
First Prize in Limited Competition 1995

Teodoro Roviralta.
Renovation of two Villas to House the
Firms Office.
Barcelona, Spain.
Construction 1995-99

Adidas Stadium.
Shopping Complex.
Paris, France.
Limited Competition 1995

1994

Cultural Complex "Mellin".
Leisure Buildings Located in
an Old Mine.
Saarbrücke, Germany.
Project 1994

Hung-Kuo Building.
Cinemas, Shopping Mall and
Residential Towers.
Shanghai, China.
Project 1994-95

Recycling Plant for Tyres.
Barcelona, Spain.
Project 1995-96

Cosmo Hall.
Ceremony Halls and Buffet-Restaurant
in the World Trade Center Building.
Osaka, Japan.
Construction 1995

1993

Schirn Café and Pavilion Annex.
Schirn Kunsthalle.
Frankfurt, Germany.
Construction 1993

Murasaki River Hotel.
Restaurant, Cinemas, Retail Areas
adjacent to New Urban Public Spaces.
Kita-kyushu, Japan.
Project 1993-94

Spin.
Revolving Panoramic Hall of the
Oriental Pearl Tower.
Shanghai, China.
Construction 1994-95

1992

Acuarinto.
Childrens Experimental and Play Park.
In collaboration with Javier Mariscal.
Nagasaki, Japan.
Construction 1992-93

Furest.
Interior Renovation of a Fashion Store.
Rambla Catalunya, Barcelona, Spain.
Construction 1992

Sceneries and Architectural Elementes.
Opening/Closing Ceremonies
Olympic Games Barcelona '92, Spain.

Gran Velvet.
Macro Discothèque and Concert Hall.
Montigalà, Badalona, Barcelona, Spain.
Construction 1992-93

1991

Disco Hall and Aparthotel.
Empuriabrava, Girona, Spain.
1991

Nuova Fiabilandia.
Amusement Park.
Rimini, Italy.
First Prize in Limited Competition.
1991

European Building.
Retail and Multipurpose Building.
European Village.
Osaka, Japan.
1991

Twin Dome.
Retail and Multipurpose Building.
Fukuoka, Japan.
International Limited Competition.
1991

Segovia Interior Design of a
Golf Club House.
Chiyoda, Tokyo, Japan.
Construction 1991-92

Estandard.
Bar, Restaurant, Club.
Barcelona, Spain.
Construction 1991-93

1990

Torres de Ávila.
Bar
In collaboration with Javier Mariscal.
Poble Espanyol, Barcelona, Spain.
Construction 1989-90

Medinaceli.
Renovation of a 19th Century Palace
into the Headquarters of a Shipping
Company.
Barcelona, Spain.
1990-94

Concert and Multiuse Hall.
Lleida, Spain.
1990-91

Neones Café.
Harajaku, Tokyo, Japan.
1990

Tokyo Time Tower.
Multiuse Building.
Nishi-Azabu, Tokyo, Japan.
1990

Manila Disco Europa.
Intervention in collaboration with
Albus, Vedrine and Coates.
Florence, Italy.
1990

Spanish Pavilion Exhibition.
Frankfurt Book Fair.
First Prize in Limited Competition.
Construction 1991

Urban Planning Bella.
Mar-Mas de la Mel.
Tourist Village.
Calafell, Tarragona, Spain.
1990

Sanson.
Panoramic Hall, Bar and Gallery in a
Former Cement Plant.
Barcelona, Spain.
First Prize in Limited Competition.
1990-91

Marugame Hirai Museum.
Contemporary Spanish Art Museum
and Office Building.
Marugame, Japan.
1991-93

1989

Sapporo Tower.
Multicomplex Building.
Sapporo, Japan.
Limited Competition.
1989

The Barna Crossing.
Culture Complex. Hotel Il Palazzo.
Fukuoka, Japan.
1989

Wind Monument.
Plaça Catalunya. Roses, Girona, Spain.
1986 and 1991

Warehouse. Grupo Rosa.
Barcelona, Spain.
1989-90

Clik dels Nens.
Children Hall.
Science Museum of Barcelona, Spain.
1989

1988

Science Museum.
Barcelona, Spain.
Fist Prize in Limited Competition.
1988

Furest Shop.
Boulevard Rosa Pedralbes.
Barcelona, Spain.
1988-89

Louie Vega.
Macro-Discotheque.
Tarragona, Spain.
1988

Gambrinus.
Restaurant. Moll de la Fusta.
Barcelona, Spain.
1988

1987

Velvet Bar.
Barcelona, Spain.
1987

Electra Shop.
Barcelona, Spain.
1987

Francisco Valiente.
Shop.
Madrid, Spain.
1987

1986

Network Café.
Barcelona, Spain.
1986-87

L'Hort de les Monges.
Barcelona, Spain.
1986-87

Pastor Private House.
Barcelona, Spain.
1986-87

Elisava.
School of Design.
Barcelona, Spain.
1986

Born in Barcelona in 1954.

Received his degree in architecture in 1977 from the Barcelona School of Architecture (ETSAB).

Professorship at ETSAB from 1978 to 1990 and from 1995 to 1996. Director of the Department of Interior Design at the Elisava School of Design from 1979 to 1989.

President of INFAD (Interior Design Association of FAD) from 1982 to 1985. Vice president of FAD (Arts and Crafts Association) from 1986 to 1988.

Established Alfredo Arribas Arquitectos Asociados in 1986.

Awards

2000 First prize. Maremàgnum extension. Barcelona harbor. Barcelona, Spain.

1998 First prize. Schwarzenbergplatz. Vienna City Council. Vienna, Austria.

1998 First prize. Hotel Peninsula. Jakarta, Indonesia.

1997 First prize. Musée Cité des Musiques Vivantes. Mairie de Montluçon, Montluçon, France.

1995 First prize. New lounges for Lufthansa German Airlines.

1995 First prize. MCC sales centers and showrooms. 100 European cities. Collaboration with Marcià Codinachs and Miguel Morte.

1994 Good Design Lighting Award of Japan. Hirai Marugame Contemporary Art Museum. Marugame, Japan.

1994 Japan Commercial Space Design Award. Hirai Marugame Contemporary Art Museum. Marugame, Japan.

1994 Kagawa Society of Architects and Building Engineers Award. Hirai Marugame Contemporary Art Museum. Marugame, Japan.

1992 Honorable mention. Bonaplata Award for New Industrial Development. Nave Rosa, Mercabarna. Barcelona, Spain.

1991 First prize. Spanish Book Fair Pavilion. Frankfurt, Germany.

1991 First prize. Nuova Fiabilandia entertainment park extension. Rimini, Italy.

1990 First prize. Extension and renewal of the old Sanson Factory. Sant Just Desvern. Barcelona, Spain.

1990 FAD gold medal for professional career.

1989 II Biennial of Barcelona. Represented Spain in the category "Young European Architects."

1988 First prize. Extension of the Barcelona Science Museum. Barcelona, Spain.

1988 EDIM Award. Comunidad Autónoma de Madrid. Francisco Valiente Shop. Madrid, Spain. Collaboration with Eduard Sansó.

1987 FAD Interior Design Award. Network Café. Barcelona, Spain. Collaboration with Eduard Sansó.

Exhibitions

2000 *Trend Hotel*. Domotex. Hanover, Germany.

1999 *Houses*. Glasgow 1999, U.K. City of Architecture and Design. Glasgow, U.K.

1997 *Die Commerzbank am Kaiserplatz*. Deutsches Architekturmuseum. Frankfurt, Germany.

1997 *De Gaudí a los Juegos Olímpicos*. Centro Cultural del Banco Intraamericano de Desarrollo. Washington D.C., USA.

1996 *Arquitectura a Catalunya. L'era democràtica 1977-1996*. SIA. Barcelona, Spain.

1996 Cataluña: Arquitectura y Ciudad. Una visión desde el proceso proyectual. SIA. Barcelona, Spain.

1995 *Alfredo Arribas: Eine Werkmonographie*. Karmeliterkloster. Frankfurt, Germany.

1995 *Barcelona, Architectures de l'exubérance. Correspondances entre le Modernisme Catalan de 1900 et la création contemporaine*. Maison de l'Architecte. Paris, France / COAC. Barcelona, Spain.

1995 *Autografías*. Escola Tècnica Superior d'Arquitectura de Barcelona. Barcelona, Spain.

1993 *Arquitectura Catalana en el Mundo*. SIA. Chicago, USA.

1992 *Bares de Barcelona*. The Deutsches Architekturmuseum. Frankfurt, Germany.

1992 *Barcelona al Pavelló de Catalunya*. Expo '92 world's fair. Seville, Spain.

1992 *Rimini Terzo Milennio. Dal progetto al cantiere. Incontri con la città futura*. Rimini, Italy.

1991 *Itineraris d'Arquitectura Catalana. 1984-1991*. COAC. Barcelona, Spain.

1991 *New Tendencies: Barcelona*. Deutsches Architekturmuseum. Frankfurt, Germany.

1991 *Diez Años de Arquitectura Española*. Consejo Superior de Arquitectos de España. Santander, Spain.

1990 *Jeunes Architectes*. SIA. Paris, France.

1990 *Design Horizonte. Alfredo Arribas 1987-1990*. Frankfurt, Germany.

1990 *Exposition au Demi-Cercle*. Paris, France.

1990 *Metropoles 90. Barcelona-Londres-Paris-Stockholm*. Pavillon de l'Arsenal. Paris, France.

1988 *Rehabilitació i Arquitectura*. Col.legi d'Arquitectes de Catalunya. Barcelona, Spain.

Lectures and Professorships

1999 Foro Internacional del Movimiento Moderno al Fin de Siglo. Mexico City, Mexico.

1997 Städelschule. Frankfurt, Germany.

1997 Museo de Bellas Artes. University of Buenos Aires. Buenos Aires, Argentina.

1996 Universidad de Puebla. Mexico.

1996 Rotterdamesse Kunsstichting. Rotterdam, Holland.

1995 The Deutsches Architekturmuseum. Frankfurt, Germany.

1995 Rotterdamesse Kunsstichting. Rotterdam, Holland.

1994 Instituto Tecnológico de Monterrey. Monterrey, Mexico.

1993 Universidad Internacional Menéndez Pelayo. Santander, Spain.

1992 IMMA. Taipei, Taiwan.

1991 Designer Zentrum. Vienna, Austria.

1991 Architectural Association Summer School. London, U.K.

1990 Design Museum. London, U.K.

Monographies

Marugame Hirai Museum Opus (Stuttgart: Axel Menges Edition, 1996).

Alfredo Arribas Architecture and Design Works 1991-1995 (Tübingen, Berlin: Ernst Wasmuth Verlag, 1995).

Alfredo Arribas Architecture and Design Works 1986-1992 (Tübingen, Berlin: Ernst Wasmuth Verlag, 1993).

partners	*collaborators*	*photographers*

<table>
<tr><td>

Seat-Stadt Pavilion
Xavier Tragant

Feli.città
Dani Freixes
Javier Mariscal

Cité des Musiques Vivantes
Dani Freixes (museography)
Xavier Tragant

Schwarzenbergplatz
Guillaume du Malet (competition)

MCC
Marcià Codinachs

Meyer House and Paulus House
Xavier Tragant

Fun Factory
Xavier Tragant

Acuarinto
Javier Mariscal

Gran Velvet
Miguel Morte

Sanson
Miguel Morte

</td><td>

Gemma Arco
Jordi Aymerich
Euro Bellessi
Winifred Binder
Antonio Bravo
Oscar Brito
Encarna Buendia
Matteo Caravatti
Miquel Casaponsa
Alex Cazurra
Anna Claramunt
Xavier Diez
Peter Duck
Stefan Eckbert
Roberto Eleuteri
Alexandra Eltsner
Xavier Franquesa
J. Ramón García
Daniel Goldschmid
Geoffrey Grulois
Michael Heim
Falk Lippelt
Javier Macias
Adrián Mallol
David Mares
Sergi Marimon
Franz Massana
Beate Mayerhoffer
Jordi Mercader
Gemma Molas
Ellen Monchen
Jordi Moreno
Susan Mortimer
Dennis Pools
Albert Que
Cinthia Raccagni
Daniel Rackespenger
Ellen Rapelius
Ignasi Raventós
Aurora Rebollo
Lara Retondini
Pedro Luis Rocha
Nelia Rosende
Cristina Sabaté
Antonella Sgobba
Marta Soriano
Susana Thomas
Mireia Torralba
Silvia Vespasiani
Pere Vilagrassa

</td><td>

Rafael Vargas
Hisao Suzuki
Duccio Malagamba
Mihail Moldoveanou
Xavier Sansuan (Schwarzenbergplatz. Model competition)
Architektürburo Photo (Commerzbank Plaza)
AAAA Studio

</td></tr>
</table>